# THE SWANAGE RAILWAY

I0894280

HERITAGE RAILWAY GUIDE

# THE SWANAGE RAILWAY

RICHARD MARKS

PEN & SWORD TRANSPORT
AN IMPRINT OF PEN & SWORD BOOKS LTD.
YORKSHIRE – PHILADELPHIA

First published in Great Britain in 2025 by
Pen and Sword Transport
An imprint of
Pen & Sword Books Ltd.
Yorkshire – Philadelphia



ISBN 978 1 03612 238 6



A CIP catalogue record for this book is available from the British Library.



Typeset in 11.5/16 Palatino by SJmagic DESIGN SERVICES, India.

The Publisher's authorised representative in the EU for product safety is Authorised Rep Compliance Ltd., Ground Floor, 71 Lower Baggot Street, Dublin D02 P593, Ireland.
www.arccompliance.com

For a complete list of Pen & Sword titles please contact

PEN & SWORD BOOKS LIMITED
George House, Beevor Street, Off Pontefract Road, Hoyle Mill, Barnsley,
South Yorkshire, England, S71 1HN.
E-mail: enquiries@pen-and-sword.co.uk
Website: www.pen-and-sword.co.uk

or

PEN AND SWORD BOOKS
1950 Lawrence Rd, Havertown, PA 19083, USA
E-mail: uspen-and-sword@casematepublishers.com
Website: www.penandswordbooks.com

MIX
Paper | Supporting responsible forestry
FSC™ C016779

# CONTENTS

# ACKNOWLEDGEMENTS

I would like to thank all of the staff and volunteers at the Swanage Railway, particularly Gavin Johns, for their assistance in researching this guidebook and for making me feel so welcome whilst visiting the railway on research and photography trips.

I would also like to thank John Scott-Morgan for commissioning this series, of which this book is the first, and for giving me access to his photograph collection. Special thanks go to John Patrick, the collections manager at Swanage Museum and Heritage Centre, for his help in locating images of the Swanage Pier Tramway.

The photographs in this book are used courtesy of Mark Pollard, Ros Marks and Hedley Thorne, or are from John Scott-Morgan's collection. The images of the Swanage Pier Tramway are used courtesy of The Swanage Museum and Heritage Centre, whilst a small number are taken from Wikimedia Commons. The remainder were taken by the author.

All photographs are credited accordingly in the captions.

## Cover Images

Swanage Railway Train passing Corfe Castle. *Hedley Thorne*

London and South Western Railway T9 Class crossing Corfe Viaduct. *Richard Marks*

## Spine Image

Swanage Strictly Bulleid Gala. *Mark Pollard*

# INTRODUCTION

The industrial heritage of Britain is everywhere you look and is a strong link not only to Britain's industrial past but also to today's vibrant manufacturing sector. One of the most obvious, and without doubt most attractive, parts of the country's industrial past are the heritage railways. These railways, saved from extinction after the closures under British Rail during the 1960s and 1970s, preserve a lost past for us to enjoy and explore in the twenty-first century.

When Richard Trevithick's first steam locomotive moved slowly along its iron rails for the first time in 1802 at Coalbrookdale in Shropshire it started a transport revolution. The early railways had been horse drawn in the main and little had changed for centuries, but the steam locomotive would change everything. Trevithick's invention revolutionised the railways, and created the foundations for the modern rail network that is taken for granted as part of our modern society. The first public railway, the Lake Lock Railroad in Wakefield, opened in 1798. The new line provided the world's first open access railway. All Britain's other lines at the time were private industrial railways in mines and factories.

The early railways were mainly built to carry freight, mostly coal and metal ores, to nearby rivers or canals where the loads were tipped into barges or ships for onward carriage. This soon changed as both demand and the search for improved local connections saw the introduction of passenger services on Britain's slowly growing railway network. These first passenger 'trains' were often stagecoaches whose wheels had been converted to run on rails, often still horse drawn, or freight wagons in which crude benches or seats had been placed. As the nineteenth century progressed, the railway network grew and with it better passenger and freight trains began to appear. The new network covered nearly all of the country, with many places at least within walking distance of a railway station.

The growth of the railways mirrored changes in both industry and society. The new transport system, whilst not directly responsible for these changes, was an important part of the British and even the global economy. With the expansion of the rail network came the national newspapers which for the first time created a single unified country, people being able to read about the events of the day each morning. Someone in Edinburgh could read *The Times* of London, whilst someone else in Plymouth could read the *Scotsman*. The arrival of national newspapers, and magazines created celebrities. Many of the music hall and theatre performers, once known only locally, became national stars who people were desperate to see. The idea of a national tour, now possible by rail, was born as a result. Entire trains carrying theatre sets, props and the cast became an increasingly common sight on the rail network. Entertainment became open to everyone everywhere.

The advent of national sport was underpinned by the possibility for teams to travel quickly to places which would have been almost impossible to reach before, unless a long, perhaps two or three day journey was undertaken. The national football and rugby leagues thus became possible, as did the county cricket championship. Sports reports in the newspapers made cricketers, footballers and rugby players household names across the whole of the United Kingdom. Again, people would go to a match just to see the stars of the day.

No longer were towns isolated from all but their nearest neighbours. Society began to change as the railways spread across Britain. The new network created the need for a standardised British time. Most places had worked to their own local time before the arrival of a railway, Bristol's clocks showing the time a few minutes different from those in London for example. For trains to operate successfully with understandable timetables a single national time was needed. It was also important so that people wishing to catch a train didn't miss it because their timepieces were set differently to those used by the railway. Greenwich Mean Time was adopted as the standard time across Britain from 1847, and all clocks were set accordingly. Some interesting exceptions remained though. The town hall clock in Bristol continued to show 'Bristol time'. It had two minute hands, one showing Greenwich time, the other Bristol local time. The time of day was not the only change to society.

Standards of living improved as industry grew through use of railway freight services. Cheaper mass-produced products were brought into towns and cities from centres of industry such as Sheffield, Birmingham and Northampton.

The lowering of costs allowed everyone access to better food, furniture, clothing and many other items which before may have been viewed as luxuries and the domain of only the very rich. The arrival of mass-produced items changed towns in another way as retail shops became increasingly common and the once popular local markets gave way to the new High Street.

Social mobility improved as industry and rail combined to grow Britain's economy which increased the standard of living for all but the very poor. The railways and industry needed people to be literate and so educational standards at school increased. Many companies then provided not only high levels of post school education but on the job training which allowed the vast majority to aspire to something better. With high employment and increasing demand for skilled workers, people became more able to achieve higher wages and improved careers. The railways allowed the population to not only travel locally to work, but further afield in search of better positions elsewhere in the country.

The railways continued to be one of the foundations of huge changes in Britain until the Second World War. The situation changed dramatically after 1945 and by the late 1950s increased car ownership and the availability of cheaper, more capable road lorries, had begun to erode the railway's once dominant position as the king of transport. Many rural railways and even some main trunk lines became unprofitable as passengers and freight drifted away to the more convenient roads or fell victim to internal railway politics.

As the 1960s progressed and with a need to save money, rather than looking to entice traffic back onto the railways, the governments of the day looked to trim the railways down. Three consecutive transport ministers, Ernest Marples, Tom Fraser and Barbara Castle, authorised closure of many stations and even complete railway lines, disconnecting many areas from the network on which some still relied. Despite common opinion, the chairman of British Rail was not able to close anything, the infamous Beeching Report was just that, merely a report. In order to close a railway which had originally been authorised by an Act of Parliament, either an Abandonment Act or an authorisation from the Minister of State for Transport has to be provided, otherwise the line and stations must remain open and be provided with a train service which at least provides a minimal number of trains per day.

A by-product of the rapid closures of many of Britain's railways in the 1960s and into the 1970s was the rise of the preservation movement. Many people, horrified by the loss of British heritage began to get together to save what they could. Local museums began to collect more ephemera and other items which marked important local events and history connected to 'their' railway. Strongly supported campaigns, and the advent of protection of important structures through 'listing', resulted in the saving of local buildings and sites of importance which had been scheduled for demolition or for building upon. Preservationists also began to look at the railways following the successful takeover of the Ffestiniog narrow gauge railway in Wales by a group of enthusiasts and businesspeople in 1954. Small groups got together to raise enough money to buy a redundant locomotive directly from British Rail as steam was being replaced by modern diesel and electric traction. Some formed larger groups who purchased more than one locomotive and formed the nascent railway societies. Other groups began to look at the possibility of saving a short stretch of railway, or even an entire branch line. After all, where were the increasing number of privately owned steam engines to be kept and run? Other groups began to look at saving coaches and freight wagons to preserve the entire railway, in a small way, which provided the rolling stock you may well travel in should you visit the Swanage Railway.

A decision made by the British Railways Board in the 1960s to quickly dispense with steam traction in favour of more modern diesel and electric locomotives, at the time greeted with horror by the preservationists, may have been one of the best things that happened to Britain's railway heritage. So many locomotives were made redundant in a short period of time that the railway workshops were unable to cope with the sheer volume of engines that needed to be cut up for scrap. The railway thus turned to the private scrapyards, selling the locomotive fleet for just the scrap value of the metals. Whilst many scrapyards bought only a few steam locomotives, which were almost immediately scrapped, some, such as Dai Woodham's on Barry Island in Wales purchased hundreds which were stored whilst the yard scrapped the more profitable redundant freight wagons. The lines of rusting hulks at Barry provided a valuable resource of which the preservation pioneers took advantage.

A large proportion of the steam locomotives that can be seen on Britain's heritage railways today were saved through purchases made from Barry and occasionally direct from British Rail. The diesel locomotives, once the source of horror, themselves became the subject of preservation attempts. The first generation of diesels were often quickly dispensed with by British Rail once the traffic for which they had been designed disappeared. More modern traction has recently become the target of groups wishing to preserve Britain's railway heritage. These locomotives have become useful additions to many heritage railway's traction fleets.

The closures of so many railway lines, hurried rejection of steam, and the first generation of diesel locomotives, provided a rich source of opportunity from which today's heritage railways have risen, phoenix-like, from the ashes. The Swanage Railway which this book explores was one of those, and without the efforts of those pioneering people who saw the value of our history, Britain's historical heritage would be so much the poorer.

This book is the first volume in a series of guide books which aim to provide a helpful accompaniment to a visit not only to Britain's heritage railways, but also to allow you to explore the heritage of the area around them.

There is much more to a heritage railway than just a ride on the train, even if it is steam hauled. In fact, some of the diesel locomotives that you may see working or parked waiting their turn, are older than some of the more modern British Railways steam locomotives !

The history and natural environment of the area through which the railway passes can be as interesting as the train itself. Britain's heritage lines often provide a very varied view out of the train window, from industrial landscapes to beautiful and idyllic rural scenes, often on the same line just a mile or two apart. Passing castles, quintessentially British villages, farms, seaside beaches, carefully restored railway stations and many other interesting scenic vistas a trip along one of Britain's heritage railways can give you a glimpse into the past, and how our ancestors lived, worked and travelled. There is much more about the heritage railway than just the train.

Railways were built for a reason, and sadly closed for a reason too as has already been outlined. This book aims to provide you, the visitor, with a handy guide to help you explore the history of the local area and the railway's place in it as well as all the fabulous collections of painstakingly restored engines, carriages, wagons and stations which you may see on the line. It also hopes to allow you to see not only Britain's rich historical heritage but also to appreciate the rich ecological sites alongside and near to the railway. Many of the heritage railways you may visit travel through sites of special scientific interest or natural importance. A railway is a very ecologically friendly way to visit these places.

The railway also provides a green corridor, the land either side of the tracks making up valuable habitats for wildlife and plants.

Why not stay longer and see more of the area rather than just have a ride on the train? Using a heritage train is a relaxing and enjoyable way to explore a part of Britain which you may not have visited before as well as being more environmentally friendly than using the car. The final section of this guide provides you with some suggested places which might be good to visit and are close to the railway.

There is much to see which may not be obvious, or may even be right on the doorstep of one of the railway's brilliantly restored stations but not visible from the train necessarily. Hop off the train and have a look around, you never know what you might find.

Perhaps visit again another time and explore more of what the area has to offer, with so much to see, one visit may not be enough to fully appreciate everything. The towns and villages along heritage lines often have a great selection of pubs and restaurants, places to visit, and great local shops and artisan workshops. Why not support local craftspeople who make fantastic products which might be just what you've been looking for, or that special gift for someone?

There is more to Britain's heritage railways than just the trains, enjoy your visit.

# GETTING TO THE RAILWAY

The Swanage Railway is located on the Isle of Purbeck, which isn't actually an island, to the south of Wareham in Dorset. The area is easily accessible by both road and public transport and if you would like something different there are also some unusual ways to reach the railway by water transport as well.

Any changes to the information that follows can be found on the Swanage Railway website in the travel pages under the 'your visit' tab.

## Getting there by road

The railway is easily reached by road, although parking in Swanage itself can be limited and traffic through the small villages on the main road from Wareham to Swanage can occasionally be quite slow as the road is very busy.

The ideal way to reach the railway by car is to travel past Wareham and park at the award-winning Purbeck Park car park at Norden. The car park is located just off the main A351 Wareham to Swanage Road (post code BH20 5DW) and is well signposted. Taking a left turn off the A351 from Wareham, to the right if approaching from the Corfe Castle and Swanage direction, and crossing the railway level crossing, the car park is located on the right. Note that the car park is not open 24 hours, and will be closed and locked in the evening; the time that it will close is clearly marked on the boards at the entrance to the car park from the road. Do check this on the Swanage Railway's website in case of changes for special events.

The car park, operated by Dorset Council, is very reasonably priced and has 350 parking spaces and well equipped toilets. Parking charges apply between 8am and 6pm, although this may change but will be clearly indicated on the parking charge boards in the car park.

to Blandford
to Wimbor
To Dorchester
A35
To Wool,
Bovington Tank Museum
Monkey World
Lulworth
Weymouth
A351
Poo
Qua
Wareham
Station
Poole Harbour
Brownsea
Island
A352
Wareham
Worgret
Junction
A351
Norden
Station
Corfe
Castle
Station
P
SR
SR
Herston Halt
P
SR
SR
Harmans Cross
Station
Chapmans Pool
Dancing Ledge
St Aldhelm's or St Alban's

*Reproduced with the permission of the Swanage Railway Company*

More details of the car park, charges and facilities can be found on Dorset County Council's website under 'Countryside, coast and parks' then following the links to Country Parks and Visitor Centres. The details of Purbeck Park can be found at the bottom of the page.

The Swanage Railway's Norden station is located just a few minutes' walk through the amenity building, turning left at the children's playground, onto a path and passing through a pleasant small wood. The path gives level access on to the station platform and ticket office. The path is well kept and suitable for all even in bad weather, although care should always be taken when the paths are particularly wet.

Whilst at Norden you may want to visit the Purbeck Mining Museum, which is located on your left as you walk along the path. The museum is not open on every day the railway is operating, so before you visit it is worthwhile to check their website or leaflets for opening times. See the section of this book on Norden for more details.

**The children's** playground at Norden behind the Purbeck Park building. The playground is provided by Dorset Council. The path to Norden station is to the left. *Richard Marks*

There is no parking available at Corfe Castle station itself, the small car park is gated off and reserved for volunteers and staff. Pedestrian access is easy via the pavement alongside Station Road which is open through the car park and into the station booking hall. Parking is very limited in Corfe Castle village itself. There are two car parks in the village, one adjacent to the A351 at the National Trust visitor centre (Post Code BH20 5DR), but this is usually quite busy and involves a walk of approximately one mile to reach the railway station. The route would involve crossing the busy A351 twice due to the arrangement of the pavements.

The second car park in the village is located on West Street (Post code BH20 5HH) and is operated by Dorset County Council. It also gets quite busy during peak holiday periods. The car park is located approximately half a mile from the station and involves a walk along Hollands Close and West Street to reach the centre of Corfe Castle from where you can cross the A351 and proceed along Station Road to reach the railway station.

The car parks in Corfe Castle are often full, especially during holiday times, and it may be difficult to find a space. It is recommended that you use the car

**Corfe Castle** seen from the National Trust visitor centre. *Richard Marks*

park at Norden instead, even if intending to visit Corfe Castle which can be done by taking a break on the journey to Swanage.

Herston Halt station has no parking facilities and is only accessible on foot from Washpond Lane. The station is approximately a twenty-minute walk from the centre of Herston. Remember that if you are intending to catch the train from or to Herston for a walk, trains do not call at the station unless by request. More details can be found in the section about Herston which follows later in this guide.

Harman's Cross station (post code BH19 3EB), has a small 50-space public car park, not run by the railway, which may prove useful. It is operated by Harman's Cross parish council and it located opposite the village hall. Payment is by an honesty box located at the entrance and there is no facility for card payments. Check the Swanage Railway's website before travelling in case of changes to access during events. It is better to park at Norden, leaving the car there, and travelling by heritage train to Harman's Cross is recommended.

There is no parking directly adjacent to the railway station in Swanage. The station forecourt is reserved for buses and taxis only. The adjacent supermarket car park is not recommended as the parking time is limited and not suitable for a day on the railway.

There are a few public car parks in Swanage itself, but parking is often limited due to the popularity of the seaside town with visitors and shoppers, especially during the summer holiday season and during the Swanage Regatta weeks. The car parks in Swanage are operated by Swanage Town Council and are considerably more expensive than Purbeck Park at Norden, if you can find a space. The nearest car park to Swanage railway station is located in Victoria Avenue at the end of the A351 (Post code BH19 1PW). The car park is approximately half a mile from the station. Exiting the car park, turn right down Northbrook Road. Follow Northbrook Road and then turn left into Gilbert Road which follows the line of the railway opposite the station. Head to the end of the road and turn right to get to the station forecourt. There are good photo opportunities of the railway along Gilbert Road.

Details of the car parks in Swanage and the charges for using them can be found on the Swanage Town Council website. Follow the link to 'Car Parks & Residents Parking Permits' from the menu on the left of the home page. All of the facilities operated by the council are listed there.

It is much better, and often quicker, to leave the car at Norden and use the railway service to reach Swanage.

## Travelling to the Swanage Railway by train

The closest National Rail station can be found at Wareham. The station is served by frequent services from and to London, Basingstoke, Bournemouth, Poole, Southampton, Weymouth, and Winchester. Connections at Basingstoke, Southampton and Bournemouth allow the traveller to reach much of the rest of the country conveniently at most times. Visitors intending to travel by rail should check the national rail website or train operators for service updates, times and fares before travelling to Wareham.

The Swanage Railway, whilst linked to the national railway network, does not operate a service from the station at Wareham currently. A two year trial period, interrupted by the Covid Pandemic of 2020, of summer shuttle services to Norden from Wareham was found to be uneconomic to operate, although these may recommence at some point in the future should funding become available to support the service. Check the Swanage Railway website news pages for updates.

**The steam** engine at the left masquerading as 80146 is 80104 taking on the identity of a long scrapped classmate. The maroon diesel locomotive (a class 37) is at one end of the service from Wareham during the trial season of mainline connection trains. *Mark Pollard*

Norden station is approximately five miles from Wareham station, and although there are pleasant walks or cycle routes across the Hartland Moor National Nature Reserve which will get you to Norden in a couple of hours, these are not for everyone. A regular bus service is provided from Wareham station which passes Norden station.

## From Wareham to Norden and Swanage by bus

Frequent bus services connect Wareham station and Wareham town to Norden and Swanage stations on the Swanage Railway. Services are operated by Morebus at the time of writing, the bus operator's website details fares and timetables which is worth checking as these vary according to the time of year. Note that the bus operator refers to the Purbeck Park Car Park as 'Norden Park and Ride'.

Service updates and travel planners can be found on the operator's website.

The No. 40 'Purbeck Breezer' bus route from Wareham railway station does not currently call at the Purbeck Park car park at Norden, the nearest stop is at Norden Farm on the A351 close by. The bus leaves from a bus stop at the rear of the station near the roundabout on Sandford Road A short walk from the bus stop will see you reach the railway station at Norden. Upon leaving the bus, head in the Swanage direction following road signs to the railway and Purbeck Park car park, being careful of traffic on the side road cross railway level crossing and enter the Purbeck Park car park on the right, proceeding through the amenities building and along the path to the station.

The No. 35 'Campsite Connect' which runs between Wareham Forest Tourist Park and Swanage calls at Purbeck Park. The bus leaves from the bus stop at the rear of the railway station, and also calls at the bus stop outside the Post Office building in Wareham town centre before heading to Norden and on to Swanage.

A short walk into town gives access to another bus route calling at Norden car park, the No. 30 'Jurassic Breezer' which runs between Weymouth and Swanage. The bus leaves from the bus stop in front of Wareham post office building and calls at the Purbeck Park car park bus stop adjacent to the amenity building in the car park.

If you prefer to start your journey on the railway in Swanage just remain on the bus as they call at the forecourt of the Swanage Railway's station in the town.

Operators may change where buses stop due to roadworks and other exceptions, so be sure to check on the Swanage Railway website or with your bus driver for updates before travelling.

## Getting there by sea

To add a slightly different experience to your journey it is possible to reach the railway by sea. If you would like to do this, drive to Sandbanks in Bournemouth and join the chain ferry which will take you across Poole Harbour to Studland from where you can drive to Corfe Castle. Leaving the ferry, follow the signposts to Corfe Castle along Ferry Road and then the B3351 which will take you to the A351. Passing under the railway bridge, turn right and head to Norden to park at the Purbeck Park car park.

The ferry runs regularly throughout the day, although on occasion the service is withdrawn in October or November for maintenance on the ferry, typically every

**Rebuilt West** Country Class, 34028 *Eddystone* crossing Corfe Viaduct with a service to Norden. Norden station is half a mile from Corfe Castle station out of sight to the left. The image was taken from within the castle. There are many vantage points where photographs can be taken from within the castle which can include the Medieval castle stone work and passing trains in the same image. *Richard Marks*

two years. There may be additional times when the ferry may not be running due to bad weather or other reasons. There is a charge for cars and pedestrians.

For tolls and service updates check the Sandbanks Ferry website before travelling.

At certain times of year, it is possible to cruise along the coast from Poole to the pier at Swanage where you can disembark and walk the short distance to the railway station for a return trip on the train before rejoining the ship to return to Poole. The coast cruise is operated by a separate company and additional charges apply and sailing times vary; the company that runs the cruises recommends the earliest sailings which will allow time to be spent in Swanage or Corfe Castle before returning. The cruise experience includes the cruise and a Swanage Railway ticket. It is recommended that sailing times and prices be checked via the Sea Train Adventure link on the directions and parking page under the 'your visit' tab of the Swanage Railway's website as these vary.

Alternatively check on the Coastal Cruises Poole Limited website page dedicated to the Poole cruises.

Note that the service does not run all year and that the operator may suspend the service due to operational constraints. Queries regarding the sea cruise should be directed to the cruise company rather than the Swanage Railway.

# A BRIEF HISTORY OF THE ISLE OF PURBECK AND THE SWANAGE RAILWAY

The Isle of Purbeck, located south of Wareham, isn't really an island. It is a peninsula surrounded on three sides by water. The English Channel laps against the eastern and southern coasts, whilst the north is cut off by the marsh lands of the River Frome and Poole Harbour. Nevertheless, it is a beautiful part of southern England which is really worth a visit or two, or even more. The area has been designated an area of outstanding natural beauty, a title which is well deserved.

The Swanage Railway has three sections which pass through areas of special scientific interest and alongside the Purbeck Heath National Nature Reserve where all six native species of reptile can be found. The railway takes its commitment to looking after the natural environment seriously, and so the lineside vegetation is not cleared during the season when birds and insects will be nesting. When it is necessary to tidy up the edges of the railway to keep the line safe, it is done sympathetically. The railway is not only a great way to travel, it is more environmentally friendly than using the car. The railway also forms a green corridor through Purbeck in which plants and wildlife can thrive.

Purbeck has a long and interesting history of human occupation. The area has a variety of Roman sites which have been excavated, some of the artefacts from which can be found in local museum collections. The town of Wareham was an important part of Anglo-Saxon Britain, one of the key towns across south and west England. Wareham was a burh, a fortified town, used not only as a place of refuge from invaders such as the Vikings, but also as a centre of government and trade. Located at the point which the Isle of Purbeck links to the rest of modern Dorset, Wareham was also a key strategic point. Anyone controlling the town also controlled the roads and waterways into Purbeck and could thus stop an army in its tracks on its defences or tax traders passing into and out of the peninsula. Many of the churches in Purbeck have their origins in the Saxon period with a Norman replacement on the site. Wareham's St. Martin's on the Walls built in 1030 is one such building.

Wareham was not the only strategic point in Purbeck. The gap in the Purbeck Ridge at Corfe provided a good access link to the port at Swanage as well as access to the local rich deposits of ball clay, Purbeck stone and Kimmeridge shale. The geology of the area resulted in a large natural mound in the valley between the steep hills either side. The mound provided an ideal place to construct a castle to defend and monitor the surrounding countryside. Castles were not just a military fortification, they were often the seat of local political power and a base for taxation of goods being transported through the area, although this varied over time.

**Corfe Castle** keep standing as an ever watchful guardian over the village. *Richard Marks*

The first 'castle' at Corfe was likely to have been Anglo-Saxon, although as little remains of the original fortification, the lack of historical evidence means it is not possible to be certain. It is highly likely that some form of fortification existed at Corfe since it is well documented that the Saxon king Edward the Martyr was murdered there in 978. The king's visit suggests that some form of castle was present at the time. The ruins that remain today are the final elements of the castle which was built to replace the probable Anglo-Saxon fortification. The Normans embarked on a programme of castle building across Britain following the Battle of Hastings, a programme the like of which would not be seen again until the time of Edward I (1272-1307). The first Norman castle on the site was undoubtably of the simple motte-and-bailey form favoured by the new rulers of Britain after 1066. The designs, seen all over Britain, consisted of a mound, the motte, on top of which stood a simple wooden or stone fortified keep. The motte was surrounded by a fortified walled courtyard, the bailey. The bailey was then surrounded by a deep ditch with a wooden palisade to act as a further layer of defence.

In some places the motte was artificially built up for a new castle, but the landscape at Corfe provided a ready-made mound on which to build a motte-and-bailey castle. Corfe Castle appears to have been one of the earliest castles in Britain constructed entirely from stone, many of the others initially being built from wood. The area is rich in good quality building stone, which meant that the builders had a ready supply of materials from which to build a strong and impressive fortification.

The arrangement of these castles was improved upon over time, and that at Corfe was no different. Stronger walls, towers and gatehouses were added to improve the strength of the fortification. All of these, as well as the original arrangement of the Norman castle upon which successive improvements have been built, can clearly be seen at Corfe Castle, even in its ruined state today.

The castles became an important symbol of wealth and political power until they became redundant after the advent of gunpowder artillery which could stand off and pound the walls until they were breached. The location of Corfe Castle, once its strength, became a liability. The overlooking ridge provided an excellent point on which to install cannons to systematically bombard the walls with little response being possible from within the castle. This proved the castle's ultimate downfall during the English Civil War when the Parliamentarian forces did just that whilst besieging the fortress.

The Isle of Purbeck has a wealth of industrial heritage as well as its impressive architectural gems. The area was a source for the much sought after Purbeck stone, which was quarried from many points across the region. There are plentiful deposits of good quality limestone which has been an important building material since the Middle Ages. Purbeck also has deposits of a particularly hard limestone, Purbeck Marble, which, whilst not geologically a form of marble, when polished takes on the appearance of it. Purbeck Marble can be found in many of the cathedrals across the whole of Britain.

The stone was quarried, or more often mined, from across Purbeck, with the majority of quarries being situated around Worth Matravers, Langton Matravers and Swanage. Often quarried from cliffs, leaving artificial caves such as those at Tilly Whim, the stone blocks were taken from the quarries and mines to the coast by horse drawn carts and on to ships at Swanage. Some mines were located right on the coast, from which the stone was loaded directly onto ships for transport by sea. The stone was used in construction from the Middle Ages and created a large and profitable industry in Purbeck.

The area also has huge deposits of ball clay around Norden, which is particularly white in colour. These have been mined for thousands of years. The clay was particularly valuable to the pottery industry, and as such the resources in Purbeck became increasingly mined during the eighteenth and into the nineteenth century. The industrial revolution saw great strides being made in the mechanisation and mass manufacturing or pottery in and around Stoke on Trent. Companies such as Wedgewood and Spode became household names, but in order to manufacture so many mass-produced homewares and ornaments, the factories needed good quality raw materials.

The ball clay from Purbeck thus became increasingly important. The clay mines increased in size in response to demand but needed to find a better way to send their produce out to the mine's customers in the midlands. The jetties built at coastal mines were fine, but the inland mines had only poor local roads to get the clay to the ships on the coast at Arne, Goathorn, Swanage and many other places where piers had been built to service small coastal ships. Something better was desperately needed, but there was an answer.

The solution to the problem was the first railway built in Dorset. In order to fulfil the orders received from Josiah Wedgewood, the Middlebere Plateway (later renamed the Middlebere Tramway) was built in 1806 by B. Fayle and

Company. The plateway connected the ball clay mines around Corfe Castle and Norden to a wharf on Middlebere Creek in Poole Harbour.

The iron plates on which the horsedrawn wagons travelled were later replaced by iron rails allowing the use of steam and later diesel locomotives. As ball clay mining continued to grow in the area, more tramways were opened to link the mines to the sea. The Furzebrook Railway (1840), Newton Tramway (1854), and Fayle's Tramway (1907) added to the Middlebere Tramway to create an intensive network of light railways around Norden and Corfe Castle.

The Isle of Purbeck, despite its mineral wealth and agricultural produce, was bypassed by the national railway network during the period of mainline railway building in the early Victorian period. The London and South Western Railway (L&SWR) bypassed the area, the nearest point it reached being Wareham on the Southampton and Dorchester Railway, operated by the L&SWR , which continued from Dorchester to terminate at Weymouth. The line was built to reach the county town, Dorchester, and the port of Weymouth. Weymouth was particularly attractive to the L&SWR since most of the fruit and vegetable produce from the Channel Islands as well as all of the wine traffic from France

**Eldon's Sidings** at Norden on Fayle's Tramway. 16 October 1962. The small diesel locomotive had replaced steam working on the mineral line. *Richard Green*

arrived in Britain at Weymouth. As such the company was keen to exploit the traffic opportunities the port offered. Its great rival the Great Western Railway also had a line to Weymouth which provided extra impetus for the line. The Southampton and Dorchester Railway was absorbed to become part of the L&SWR in 1848.

The line opened in 1847 with the station at Wareham opening at the same time. The current station is a replacement on the same site dating from 1887.

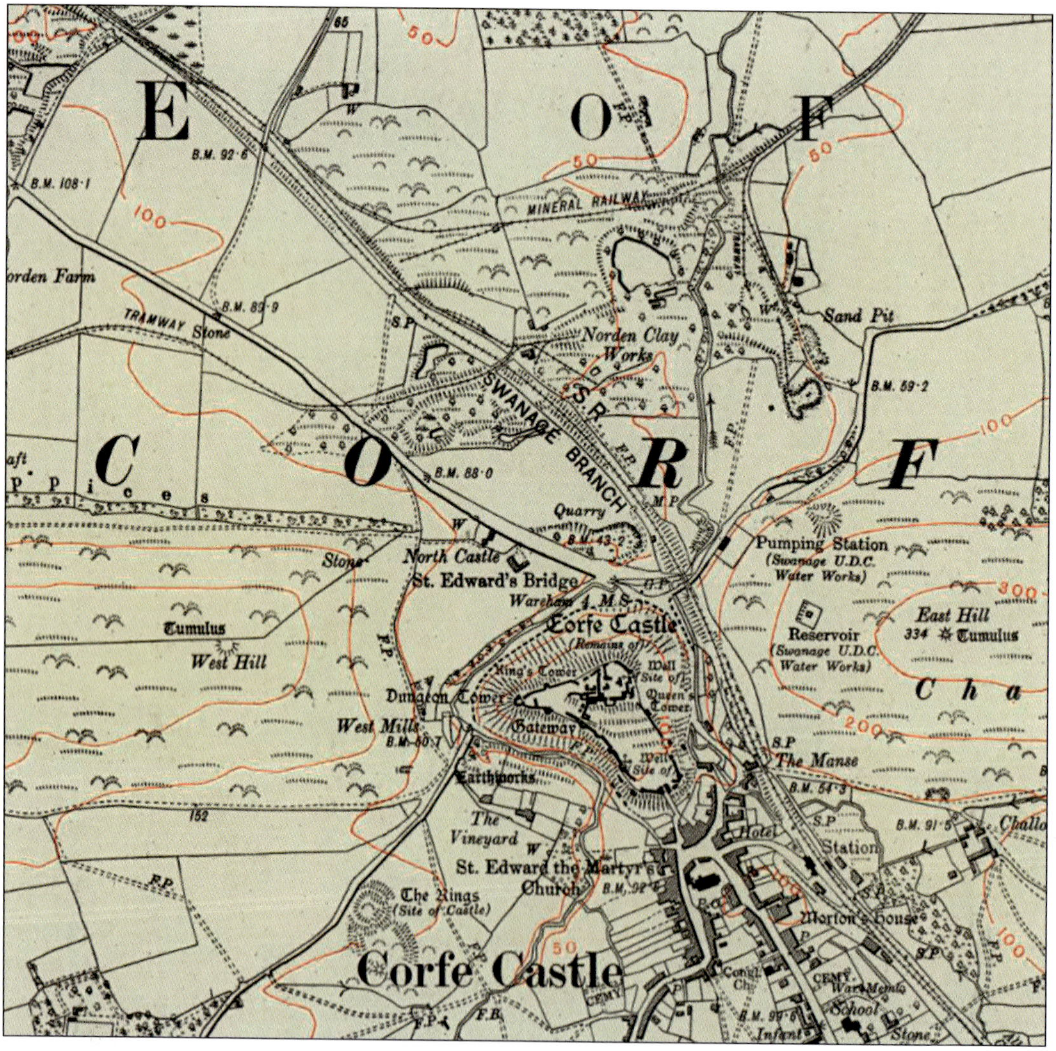


**Corfe Castle** in 1929. The mineral railways around the site of the modern Norden station are clearly marked. Purbeck Park car park and the Purbeck Mining Museum are on the site of Norden Clay Works. Ordnance Survey, Dorset LVI.NW (includes: Church Knowle; Corfe Castle.) - Ordnance Survey Six-inch England and Wales, 1929 (nls.uk). *Reproduced with the permission of the National Library of Scotland*

The Southampton and Dorchester took a fairly circuitous route from Southampton via Wimborne and as such became known as 'Castleman's Corkscrew' after the name of the railway scheme's main promoter Charles Castleman. A cut-off line was later built from the L&SWR station at Bournemouth, through Poole to Wareham. Castleman's Corkscrew was closed to passengers between Lymington Junction and Hamworthy Junction in 1964, which left Wimborne cut off from the railway network. Freight traffic ceased on the last stub of the old line in 1977. The cut-off line is the railway which serves Wareham today.

No thought was given to the needs of Purbeck. Wareham was too far away from most of the industry of Purbeck which continued to send its mineral traffic by sea. The arrival of the railway at Wareham encouraged a succession of schemes to build a railway into Purbeck but none came to fruition due to lack of local support. Eventually a scheme was proposed which met the needs of the area much better than those which preceded it. The project gained local support and the Swanage Railway finally received its authorising Act of Parliament in 1881.

All railways need to be authorised by Parliament and have an Act passed before construction may commence. The Swanage Railway Act 1881 was passed on 18 July 1881 with a share capital of £90,000 authorised, plus the power to borrow a further £30,000. The railway appointed the engineer W.R. Galbraith to build the line, and construction began.

The railway opened in 1885 and from the start was operated on behalf of the company by the L&SWR which later absorbed the Swanage Railway Company in 1886. This was extremely common during the time of railway building. The branch line left the main line at Worgret Junction just over a mile from Wareham station. As it passed through Purbeck it crossed the existing Furzebrook Railway and Middlebere Tramway, although facilities to exchange ball clay traffic would come later. There was only a single station on the branch, located at Corfe Castle.

The branch benefitted from the local mineral traffic, the ball clay and Purbeck stone once carried by sea switching to the more flexible and convenient rail services. Local agricultural produce also helped make the branch a profitable addition to the L&SWR network.

The second period of industrial revolution during the nineteenth century saw a massive change in working conditions and reduced working hours as successive Victorian governments passed Acts of Parliament which improved

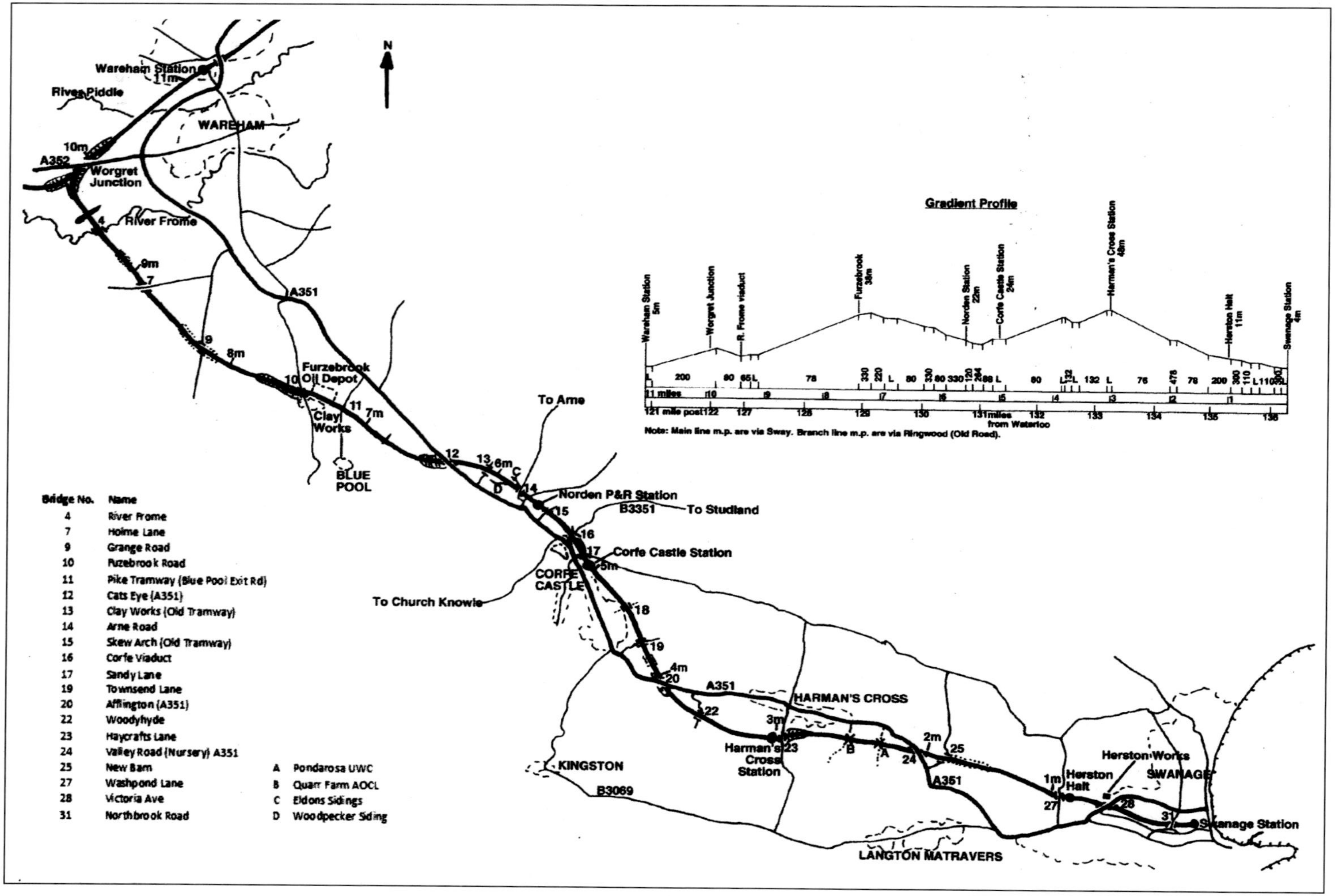


**Swanage Railway** Route Map. *Reproduced with the permission of the Swanage Railway Company*

**Norden exchange** shed. Ball clay from the Norden mines was transferred from narrow-gauge tramway wagons to BR wagons (one shown waiting), and taken to the potteries around Stoke on Trent for use in making fine china. 16 October 1962. *Richard Green*

conditions in factories and mines, as well as other workplaces. Working hours were gradually reduced until the eight hour working day with which we are familiar was put into legislation.

Swanage would benefit from this Victorian legislation and its new place on the growing national railway network. In 1802, the Health and Morals of Apprentices Act was passed which lay down that all factories must be disinfected and cleaned twice a year. The Act was followed by the Factories Act 1844 which made it mandatory for every factory to be completely cleaned with limewash every fourteen months. The advent of steam powered machinery coupled with the new legal framework under which factories operated created a need to close the factory for at least a week once a year for maintenance of the machinery and cleaning of all the buildings. The idea of a holiday was thus born and many companies began providing a company holiday or day trips by train.

Standards of living gradually rose for many people which, coupled with the new 'factory break', created a desire to escape from the industrial towns and cities. At the same time, the national newspapers and magazines distributed by rail which were full of advertisements for trips and holidays; the rise of the professional middle classes with more disposable income; a slightly more affluent working class, and the publicity produced by the railway companies to generate 'holiday' traffic on their coastal lines, combined to create the British seaside holiday. People flocked to the new seaside resorts by rail towards the end of the nineteenth century, Bournemouth and Swanage both becoming popular destinations.

During the summer, the Swanage branch was particularly busy as the development of Swanage as a holiday resort in the late nineteenth century created increased passenger traffic. Through coaches from London, the Midlands and North were detached from trains at Wareham and coupled to the branch train for onward travel to Swanage. The railway also began to run entire trains to bring holidaymakers to Swanage.

The Southern Railway took over the branch after the L&SWR was grouped into the company as a result of the Railway Act 1922 under which all of Britain's 120 separate railway companies were amalgamated into just four large companies. The Southern decided in 1937 to extend the existing station buildings.

**Swanage station** by Derek Harper

**Southern Railway** F6 class number 362 shunting the branch line freight train at Swanage. 28 August 1933. *John Scott-Morgan Collection*

The extension was sympathetically undertaken using the same materials as the original 1885 building for a design which merged seamlessly into the existing building. The new building provided an extended parcels office, booking office and waiting hall, and a newsagent's shop. At the same time, the goods shed was extended to cope with increasing freight traffic for the growing town.

The branch line would remain busy until after the Second World War. The increased availability of cheap family cars saw ownership rise, and the convenience of the roads began to impact upon railway traffic. Visitors either drove to Purbeck or went abroad after the advent of the relatively cheap package holiday during the late 1950s. The Swanage branch became increasingly unprofitable as a result, something which the nationalised British Railways, created in 1948, became increasingly concerned about.

The station at Swanage was reduced to just a single track, and only one side of the platform was used. British Rail had 'rationalised' the railway as decreasing traffic made the line uneconomic to operate so savings were sought. Only one track ran into the station, everything else was lifted, the goods yard was closed and all the sidings removed. The engine shed was also closed, disconnected and

**Branch train** for Swanage at Wareham, Dorset, 27 July 1966. *Dr Neil Clifton*

left derelict. Services continued to be operated by diesel multiple units (DMU), the steam services, latterly worked as a push-pull operation since Southern Railway days, ceasing as part of British Railways' modernisation plan.

The push-pull trains had a cab in the coach at one end of the train where the driver could control it in one direction, driving from the locomotive cab in the other. This sort of operation was quicker as the locomotive did not need to run around at each end of the journey. The DMUs which followed effectively recreated the same method of working but without a separate locomotive.

The line between Corfe Castle and Swanage was simplified and operated under the 'one engine in steam' principle (despite the train being diesel powered) which allows only a single train to be in that area at a time. The train can only shuttle back and forth along what is effectively a long siding. Signal control remained between Corfe Castle and Worgret Junction signal boxes. British Railways proposed closing the line from Wareham to Swanage in 1967 and issued notices accordingly in 1968 after receiving authority to do so from the Secretary of State for Transport. A railway cannot close a line without governmental permission; the Secretary of State for Transport, Barbara Castle, gave permission in this

**View SE,** towards Swanage: ex-LSW Wareham - Swanage branch. The train is approaching the site of the later Norden station, propelled by ex-LSW Drummond M7 0-4-4T No. 30111. *Ben Brooksbank*

case although the closure was delayed due to local protests and a department inspector who decided that the line ought to remain open. Despite the reprieve, the decision of the inspector was overturned once more and the line closed to passenger services. The last public service ran during the evening of 1 January 1972. British Rail lifted all the remaining track between Swanage and past the site of the current Norden station leaving a stub of the branch serving the oil and gas terminal at Furzebrook.

The Swanage Railway Society, after years of hard campaigning and fund raising, were given access to the site of Swanage station where the derelict station, engine shed and goods shed still fortunately remained. The preservationists were given a one year lease by Swanage Town Council which was later extended. The station was restored and track re-laid, a small group of volunteers working hard until in the summer of 1979 when the first trains were run on a short section of railway in Swanage Station.

The aim was always to connect the heritage railway back to Wareham, and over time the railway was slowly rebuilt towards Corfe Castle. Everything had

**Swanage Station** in 1985. *John Baker*.

been removed by British Rail other than the bridges, so the new company had to recreate the railway from just an empty track bed. The railway reached the outskirts of Swanage in 1984, one mile from the station. A temporary halt was built there to be the first terminus of the railway although it continued to inch its way towards its goal.

A threat arose to the future of the preserved railway when during the 1980s a proposal was put forward by the council for the overgrown and abandoned track bed through Corfe Castle to be used as a possible route for a bypass avoiding the centre of the village. Fortunately, it was decided, after a public enquiry, that the track bed should be retained for the use of the railway. The railway reached Harman's Cross in 1989, where the current station was built. The village became the terminus of the line until 1995. Reconstruction continued, with the railway getting ever closer to the goal of Corfe Castle.

**Austerity tank** locomotive 'Joseph' on Swanage turntable. Originally built during the Second World War to supply the army as well as railways in Britain and, after D-Day, those in Western Europe with shunting engines, they were built in great numbers after the war. The capable and easy to maintain engines were popular in industry, being used in collieries, steel mills, breweries and many other types of factory. The qualities which made them so useful to industry and the cheap price withdrawn locomotives could be purchased for, made them key to the start of Britain's heritage railways. Joseph was important to the early days of the Swanage Railway. *Mark Pollard*

The railway could not open to Corfe Castle, despite the rails having reached the now restored station. The council agreement with the railway that allowed the line to be reopened stipulated that the line must continue to Norden where a park and ride facility would be made available on the site of an old clay mining facility. This was due to the congestion of traffic in Corfe Castle and lack of parking which would be made worse by the attraction of a steam railway in the town. The half a mile to Norden was completed and trains returned to Corfe Castle station in 1995, 24 years after the last British Rail service left the station. The Swanage Railway laid one further mile of track across the road at Norden to link up with the National Network at Furzebrook. The dream of the pioneering preservationists had been met, but that is only the beginning of the story…

# THE RAILWAY STATIONS AND OTHER THINGS TO DO

## Norden

Norden station was built by the Swanage Railway as the terminus to its services, adjacent to the park and ride facilities provided by Dorset Council. As part of the agreement allowing the railway to extend back to Corfe Castle, and in consideration of the lack of car parking in Corfe Castle, the railway agreed to extend the short distance past Corfe Castle. The station is new and was built by the railway as the terminus of the line's heritage services. The station was located at Norden to allow visitors to arrive at the Purbeck Park car park rather than attempting to park in Corfe Castle.

There is much more to Purbeck Park than just somewhere to leave the car for the day. The main building adjacent to the car park is well equipped with lavatories. Next to the facility building there is, at the time of writing, a cycle hire company where you can rent a bicycle or two and set off to explore the ecologically rich Hartland Moor National Nature Reserve. Opposite the buildings you will find a wooden play area with a railway theme where you can let the kids burn off some of that energy they've built up in the car on the way. Turning to the left, the tree lined path takes you to Norden Station, but why not stop for a while at the Purbeck Mineral and Mining Museum on the left as you head to the station?

A visit to the mining museum is highly recommended if it is open and you have time before your train. If not, why not come back another time to learn about Purbeck's rich mining heritage? The Purbeck mining industry was an important source of traffic for the Swanage branch and a visit to the museum is a valuable part of a trip to the railway.

**Narrow gauge** tramway bridge over Swanage branch. 16 October 1962. The remains of the bridge can still be seen today at the Corfe Castle end of the platform at Norden station. *Richard Green*

The museum is accessed through the gates to the side of the path, but is not open every day. It is usually open on Tuesday, Wednesday and Thursday as well as on Saturday and Sunday between 11:00am and 4:00pm, with last entry being at 3:30pm during the summer months. Check the Purbeck Mining Museum website for more details as opening days and times vary during the summer, and the museum often has reduced opening hours during the winter months.

The Purbeck Mining museum is an independent museum and educational charity dedicated to preserving anything related to the history of the Purbeck Ball Clay mining industry, the narrow gauge railways which used to transport the clay and clay mining's association with the Swanage branch. The collection held by the museum includes mining equipment used in the ball clay mines, as well as artefacts associated with the social and economic history of the area.

Ball clay is a rare commodity, found only in a few places around the world. Valued for its whiteness and properties when fired it is an important material in the production of ceramic products. The Isle of Purbeck is particularly rich in the material and its value prompted mining to begin on an industrial scale in the 1600s. The clay was transported by water to Poole from where it was sent on to London and further afield. The whiteness of the clay attracted the manufacturers of pottery in the area around Stoke on Trent during the 1700s, Purbeck ball clay becoming a key ingredient in Wedgewood pottery. As a result of the new demand, an advanced mining industry was created which created a lot of local wealth and provided jobs. Benjamin Fayle created Dorset's first railway, the Fayle Tramway, to carry the clay to a wharf at Middlebere on the coast of Hartland Moor. Initially horse drawn, like many early railways, steam locomotives were introduced in the 1800s and were still being used when the extensive network of light railways closed in the 1950s. Exchange sidings were located at Norden to transfer the clay from the narrow gauge wagons into main line wagons for transport out by rail.

**Bellis &** Seeking (of Birmingham) 2ft 8.5in gauge 0-6-0WT *Secundus* (no works number) of 1874 built for the Furzebrook Tramway of Pike Bros., Fayle & Co.'s claypits in Isle of Purbeck, Dorset. *Hugh Llewelyn*

One locomotive used in Purbeck, *Secundus*, survives in the care of the museum. The narrow bridge that can be seen crossing the railway at the Corfe Castle end of Norden station was part of the extensive industrial railway network in the area. It is hoped that the bridge may one day be restored and used to extend the narrow gauge railway operated by the museum on some dates, usually coinciding with special events on the Swanage Railway.

There is a great opportunity once a week to hear from a retired clay miner who visits the museum to tell you what life was like in Purbeck's mines in the 1960s and to answer your questions. The website publicises the days when the miner is in residence. The museum also has an immersive replica mine which is well worth seeing.

There is no entry charge at the time of writing but a donation to help care for the collection would be much appreciated by the volunteers who run the museum. So why not pop in for a while and enjoy the fascinating history of clay mining in Purbeck? If you would like to see more of the industrial heritage of the area, the old Middlebere tramway track bed is now a pleasant walking route across Hartland Moor, more details of which can be found later in this heritage guide.

After you have visited the museum, continuing along the path will bring you to the Swanage Railway. The platform and booking office are to the left via an accessible ramp. The area to the right is a good place to watch the locomotive running around its train ready to go back to Swanage. To the right you can see the railway carrying on over the main road via the level crossing you passed over to get into Purbeck Park. The line disappearing into the distance is the link to the national network at Worgret Junction west of Wareham.

Services are not proceeding to Wareham in 2024 but may recommence at some point in the future if external funding becomes available. In the meantime, the link is only used to bring in rail tours and some visiting locomotives. The concrete area on the opposite side of the road is used to bring in visiting engines and to send Swanage locomotives out on loan by road.

Norden station consists of a booking office with two windows. It is worth bearing in mind that from 2024 the Swanage Railway took the decision to no longer accept cash payments. Passing the booking office with your railway tickets in hand, you will arrive on the platform. There is a refreshment kiosk on the platform which serves hot and cold drinks and delicious locally made cakes and snacks, as well as a limited hot menu at times. The kiosk is run by

**The 'end** of the line' at Norden. Currently the terminus of passenger services, the line continues past Norden station and crosses the road by the cabin in the distance on the left. The line continues to meet the national railway network at Worgret Junction. On some special event weekends trains continue to the boundary between the Swanage Railway and Network Rail. A locomotive is required at each end of the train as no run round facilities are available. *Richard Marks*

volunteers so may not be open every day. Adjacent to the kiosk can be found the station's second-hand book and magazine stall where you might just find that gem you have been looking for. All proceeds go to the upkeep of the station. The refreshment kiosk and book stall are only open on days the railway is operating, and on quieter days they may be closed as they are run by volunteers.

## Corfe Castle

Corfe Castle station was the only intermediate stop on the Swanage Branch before the line was closed by British Rail. It is fortunate that the original station buildings built in 1885 survive. This fine example of L&SWR rural station architecture, with its nearby goods shed, still survives thanks to the hard work of the restoration team to be enjoyed by visitors today. British Rail often demolished all the structures along a railway line after it was closed. The demolition teams lifting the tracks also removed any other railway equipment including signals for reuse or scrapping and frequently bulldozed buildings leaving them as just a pile of rubble. On the occasion that the buildings were left standing they were left uncared for and became derelict, and damaged by vandals and the weather. They often became dangerous and had to be demolished by the local council.

Fortunately this did not happen at Corfe Castle, although the signal box had already been removed by British Rail long before closure. The service on the line was reduced to a very basic single train shuttling between Swanage and Wareham, with the section from Corfe Castle to the terminus at Swanage being operated with only one train being allowed at a time, effectively turning the branch line into a long siding.

The station is an excellent way to reach the village, since car parking is so limited and roads very busy. Visitors travelling towards Swanage should head

**Corfe Castle** Station seen in a derelict condition in 1979. *John Lucas*/Corfe Station - derelict in 1979.

NEXT TRAIN
NORDEN ONLY

to the footbridge and cross to the other platform to exit the station. Those with pushchairs or unable to climb the stairs of the footbridge should approach a member of platform staff who will be more than happy to help you cross the line by the platform ramps and barrow crossing at the Norden end of the station once it is safe to do so.

The station has a waiting shelter on the platform for trains to Swanage next to the rebuilt signal box, whilst the main station building is on the platform for trains heading to Norden. Note though that on occasion trains may run in either direction through the main station platform.

The main station building has been sympathetically restored transporting you back to the golden age of railway travel as you step through the doors. The wooden floors and coal fires in the winter are welcoming, as is the restored

***Opposite*: Corfe** Castle Station from the footbridge over the railway. *Richard Marks*

***Below*: Corfe** Castle station on a sunny summer's day. In the background the ruins of the castle dominate the skyline, showing the important strategic location of the fortification. The castle is only a few minutes' walk from the station. *Rosalind Marks*

ladies waiting room. In the past, railways provided women only waiting rooms to ensure their safety when travelling alone, and the example at Corfe Castle is a wonderful restoration of something now lost to time. The station has toilets should you need them.

The porters' office in the station building was closed by British Rail when they dispensed with and demolished the old signal box. The office was converted into a small signal cabin with a small lever frame and single track token machine installed. Trains between Worgret Junction and Corfe Castle were controlled from the room, with those between Corfe Castle and Swanage operated without signals, only one train being permitted to be in the section. This method of working is often referred to as a 'long siding'. When the line closed in 1972 the equipment was removed by British Rail.

The Swanage Railway restored the office for use as a signal cabin when the line was reopened to Corfe Castle and on to Norden. Equipment retrieved from the national network when it was made redundant was installed, replicating

**Harman's Cross** signal box. Like the rest of the station, everything at Harman's Cross was built from nothing by the Swanage Railway. There never was a station in the village, which may seem hard to believe sitting on the platforms today. *Richard Marks*

**Corfe Castle** signal box and platform shelter on the Swanage bound (down) platform at the station. The signal box was rebuilt by the Swanage Railway on the site of the original which was demolished by British Railways. The new box is worth comparing with the original. It has been built in the more usual style with large windows giving the signaller a good panoramic views of operations, whereas the original only had small windows at the top. Since the station house is no longer a residence there is no risk of the top floor rooms being overlooked. *Rosalind Marks*

how British Rail had operated the line, but with one important difference. Corfe Castle 'signal box' only controlled the line as far as Norden but retook control of the line as far as Harman's Cross where a new signal box had also been built at the railway's station there.

A new signal box was built to replicate the original that had once stood on the opposite platform, and when opened the new facility took over control of trains between Norden and Harman's Cross in conjunction with the signal boxes located at the other two stations. The signal cabin in the main building was made redundant and decommissioned, although all the equipment was left in place to act as an immersive experience where you can learn how to be a railway signaller.

**The very** welcoming Booking Office at Corfe Castle station. *Richard Marks*

Leaving the station through the main entrance in the building or via the side gate you can choose to visit the museum and refreshment rooms, or to head off into Corfe Village. Turning left and heading into the old goods yard, which can also be accessed directly from the platform via a ramped gate at the Swanage end of the station, you approach the old goods shed, cinema coach, picnic area and refreshment room in a large railway carriage. Take a well-earned rest in the cinema coach and watch archive films about the history of the line, and its recreation by the dedicated volunteers who made everything you are enjoying on your visit in all sorts of weather. Carry on into the old goods shed which is now Corfe Castle Railway Museum. A visit is highly recommended. The museum is full of fantastic artefacts, images and documents which trace the social story of the railway and its importance to the local communities and industries which came to rely upon it. The museum is free to visit, but is only open on days that the railway is operating.

The museum book wagon parked at the Cattle Dock has a wide selection of second hand railway books, some of which can be difficult to find. All the proceeds go towards the upkeep of the museum.

**Inside Corfe** Castle railway museum. *Richard Marks*

**Another view** of the exhibitions inside the railway museum at Corfe Castle. *Richard Marks*

You may feel now you need a cup of tea or a nice coffee, so a visit to the refreshment rooms in the railway coach, which is easily accessible from the ramp and platform next to it, might be needed. The coach offers a tempting range of teas and coffees, homemade cakes as well as hot and cold food from a daily menu.

The old cattle dock platform, once used to transport livestock by rail, is now available as a picnic area. Equipped with tables and benches the dock is a great place to sit and enjoy the views of Purbeck behind the station, and the sights and sounds of passing trains, as you enjoy your picnic.

Once you are feeling refreshed a visit to Corfe Castle Village is recommended.

Heading back to the main exit from the station turn right out of the main doors, or continue straight ahead if you have come directly from the goods shed. Walking along Station Road you will reach the centre of Corfe Castle with the Bankes Arms Hotel on your right.

The road ahead of you is the A351 main road to Swanage and is very busy at most times of the day. There is a traffic-light-controlled crossing to the left in front of the village store.

**The cattle** dock at Corfe Castle station is now a picnic area. The building to the side is the old goods shed which is now a railway museum. To the left you will find the café coach. The brown goods van is the second-hand book shop which is open on certain operating days. *Richard Marks*

Crossing the road, the Church of St Edward, King and Martyr is directly in front of you. Dedicated to King Edward the Confessor (962-978) who was murdered in the village, the church is home to an alabaster altar with carvings inset in white marble. The altar was designed by the Victorian architect George Edmund Street and presented to the church by Lord Eldon in 1876.

Turning to the right will take you into the village square. At the centre of the square stands a cross commemorating Queen Victoria's diamond jubilee in 1897. The square is surrounded by shops and the Greyhound Inn.

The square has a National Trust shop which is directly ahead of you and a tearoom to your right adjacent to the entrance to Corfe Castle itself. Both are located in Grade II listed buildings.

The entrance to Corfe Castle, which is a National Trust property, can be found at the end of West Street and is clearly signposted. The ticket office is to the right, although National Trust members can continue directly across the bridge over the old moat and into the castle via the ticket checking booth in the

**Corfe Castle** keep seen from the grounds of St Edward the Martyr church. *Rosalind Marks*

gatehouse. If you wait for a moment on the bridge, you will be able to see trains passing on the railway through the trees, it makes an excellent spot for a photograph.

The first castle on the site was built by William the Conqueror in the eleventh century and dominates the gap between the hills, effectively controlling access to the rest of Purbeck. Continual rebuilding and improvements to reflect the best in military architecture changed the castle throughout the twelfth and thirteenth centuries. In 1572, the castle was sold to Sir Christopher Hatton by Elizabeth I. It was then sold on to Sir John Bankes in 1635. The Bankes family sided with Charles I during the English Civil War. Whilst her husband was away fighting for the king, Lady Mary Bankes led the defence of the castle against the Parliamentarians.

**Rebuilt Bulleid** West Country class, 34070 *Manston* passes tender first approaching Corfe Castle station from Norden. The railway passes above the roofs of the houses although the land rises steeply to meet the level of the railway afterwards. The photograph was taken through the trees, which have grown up in the castle's defensive ditch, from the bridge at the castle's entrance. *Richard Marks*

The castle survived a siege in 1643 but by 1645 it was one of the few remaining Royalist strongholds and was once more besieged. The castle was assaulted and surrendered to the Parliamentarian forces surrounding it in 1646. Corfe Castle was then deliberately destroyed by gunpowder, referred to as 'slighting' at the time, creating the spectacular ruins we can enjoy today. The ruins are a Grade I listed building recognised as an internationally important structure.

There are many vantage points in the castle ruins from which photographs of the surrounding area can be taken. On the side of the castle facing the A351, the railway passes close by offering the opportunity to capture some extremely atmospheric images of passing trains through the remains of the castle.

**Corfe Castle** village from the battlements of the castle. *Richard Marks*

More information about the castle, opening times, special events and prices can be found on the castle's page on the National Trust website. It is well worth a visit.

If instead of going to the castle you turn left and head away from it down West Street you will pass The Fox Inn on the right and come to Corfe Castle Museum on the left side of the road. The museum is located in the world's smallest townhall building, a blue plaque above the entrance confirming it as such and making for an interesting photo opportunity.

Immediately opposite the museum you will come to the entrance to Corfe Castle Model Village and café on the right. The model village is a 1:20 scale model of the castle village as it appeared in 1646 before the castle was destroyed. The model village is privately run, opening times and entry prices as well as details of the Courtyard Café can be found on the model village's website.

The public car park in Corfe Castle may be found by continuing along West Street and following the signs to the Car Park to the right.

The railway is an excellent way to visit the atmospheric open air cinema screenings at Corfe Castle which are run as part of the Purbeck Film Festival. More details about the festival can be found later in this book.

After exploring Corfe Castle it may be time to head back to the station to catch the train to Swanage.

**Corfe Castle** has more claims to fame that just the castle. It has the smallest town hall building in England, which is now partly a museum. *Richard Marks*

**West Street,** Corfe Castle. *Richard Marks*

## Harman's Cross

Harman's Cross station was built by the Swanage Railway as the heritage railway was restoring and reopening the line gradually towards Corfe Castle. The railway never had a station at Harman's Cross prior to the line's closure by British Rail. The station was opened by the Swanage Railway in 1989 as the temporary terminus for heritage train services until such time as the extension to Corfe Castle and Norden was completed. When the line was reopened past Harman's Cross, a new signal box was built to jointly control trains to Corfe Castle in one direction and to Swanage in the other. A passing loop and second platform were put in place allowing trains to pass each other on the single track branch line. Harman's Cross is now the main crossing point for trains heading to Swanage from Norden and in the opposite direction.

The buildings on the station, whilst new, have been built in the style of a L&SWR wayside station. It is almost impossible to imagine that the station never existed before the preservationists arrived to reconstruct the railway, but build it they did. The platforms are impressively provided with gardens and flower

**The beautifully** tended gardens on the Norden bound (up) platform at Harman's Cross station. Once a common sight across Britain's railways, station gardens are now relatively rare. *Richard Marks*

**The Swanage** bound (Down) platform at Harman's Cross. The large building is the booking office, although this is not open on every day the railway is operating. The exit from the station is behind the building. *Richard Marks*

beds and are well worth stopping off en route to Swanage to see if you have time. Station gardens were once a feature of Britain's railways and a source of pride to the station master and staff who worked there. Railway companies often had an annual 'best kept station' competition for which prizes were awarded to the station staff by the directors of the railway. Winning one of those coveted awards was seen as a source of immense pride to the people who worked at the station. As a result of their efforts the station is a nice place to take some time out and wait for a train instead of the rather utilitarian railway stations we often see on the national network in the twenty-first century.

There are no refreshment room facilities on the station, although both platforms have pleasant waiting rooms. The Norden bound platform has picnic benches where you could sit and enjoy the peace and quiet of a typical British wayside station located in a tranquil spot with unspoilt views of the Purbeck countryside.

The ticket office is located on the Swanage bound platform, but is not open at all times. When the booking hall is closed, tickets for travel, if not booked

**The picnic** area at Harman's Cross station. The station is a tranquil place to sit and spend some down time between trains. With scenic views across Purbeck, and local wildlife close by, the station is a peaceful haven from everyday life for a short while. *Richard Marks*

online in advance, should be purchased from the travelling ticket inspectors or the guard on board the train.

The station platforms are accessed via ramps from Haycrafts Lane. There is no footbridge or barrow crossing at the station, the only way to change platforms is to leave the station via the ramp, and cross the railway along the road bridge before returning to the platforms by the relevant rampway. The council run car park is located across the road opposite the village community centre, the entrance to the Swanage bound platform lying to the side of the centre's grounds. Entry to the Norden bound platform can be found at the opposite end of the road bridge.

Harman's Cross is located conveniently for local campsites, which are just a short walk away. For those looking for an interesting walk, there are footpaths from the station towards the south where you can enjoy stunning views of the Jurassic Coast. The remains of the mines from where Portland Stone was quarried, and one of the reasons for the construction of the railway in the nineteenth century can also be seen from the paths. A good walker's guide to the area will provide a varied selection of interesting walks suitable for everyone. Equipped with your favourite books of walks, Harman's Cross station is a great place to start your adventure.

## Herston Halt

Herston Halt station was also built by the Swanage Railway as the terminus of its early services from Swanage before the line was extended towards Corfe Castle. There was originally no station on the site, the current one only existing since the preservationists took on the line after its closure by British Rail. Herston Halt opened in 1984 as the first terminus for the Swanage Railway's heritage trains once they began to rebuild the line towards Corfe Castle. The station was originally only a short wooden platform capable of accepting a train only two coaches in length. This was, however, sufficient for the railway's nascent services. The original short wooden platform was replaced by the current concrete structure which was donated to the Swanage Railway. When the Croydon Tramlink was created in South London, parts of the old Woodside station in Croydon through which the tram line was to pass became unsuitable. The station was rebuilt and replaced by Woodside Tram stop. The old railway platforms were replaced by new tram platforms, making the old structures redundant. They were still perfectly usable and so were donated to the Swanage Railway for reuse at Herston Halt.

The station consists of a simple platform with no other facilities. It can be accessed only via a pathway from Washpond Lane and there is no car parking at the station. Despite its simple construction, the station serves as a useful connection to local campsite and walking routes.

Once the line had extended as far as Harman's Cross the halt became a request stop only. Most trains do not usually pause at the halt unless a stop is requested. If you wish to alight from a train at Herston Halt you should inform the guard on the train when you board. The guard will inform the driver who will stop the train at the platform for you.

If you wish to board a train at Herston you should give a very clear signal, as early as possible, to the driver of an approaching train that you wish them to stop so that you can travel on the train.

## Swanage

Swanage station is the original terminus of the railway branch from Wareham and we are fortunate to be able to see the original station building, albeit the extended and improved version built by the Southern Railway.

The station first opened in 1885 when the L&SWR came to Swanage. The station building is built from local Purbeck stone as are the goods and locomotive sheds visible from the end of the platform. The station has a single platform with two faces from which trains can arrive and depart. The main platform is most commonly used as it has a run round loop which allows the locomotive to change ends on the train ready to return to Norden. The second platform has no such facility and is mostly used for operating trains during special events or galas where another locomotive might be available to replace that which brought the train in from Norden for the return trip. Occasionally a train may depart from that side, but will return to the other side of the platform. The platform is otherwise used to store a second set of coaches not in use on the day.

The large building to the left, as you face the Corfe Castle direction, is the old goods shed. The shed was once part of a considerable railway goods facility which covered the area now occupied by the supermarket and doctor's surgery. One of the sidings in the yard was extended to cross the road at the end of the line. The extended line ran in a narrow alley behind the parade of shops on the right hand side of Station Road to reach a stone store near the waterfront. Purbeck stone quarried locally was brought to the store and then loaded onto railway wagons to be taken away by rail. The area is no longer used by the railway apart

**L&SWR M7** class, 30053 at Swanage. Note the coach in the other platform which is still in British Rail blue. Mixes of vintage and British Rail liveried coaches could often be seen during the early days of Britain's heritage railways. *Mark Pollard*

from the old goods shed which is now the railway's carriage restoration and maintenance workshop.

The station has an excellent souvenir and gift shop which is open every day that the railway is running. The shop stocks a wide range of souvenirs, clothing, toys and gifts suitable for all ages. There is also a good range of railway related DVDs and books as well as model railways. The shop has a range of cold drinks and sweets. Next to the railway shop, in the booking hall you will find the station kiosk selling a range of hot and cold drinks and snacks, including locally produced ice cream and cakes.

Leaving the station through the booking office, you will arrive on the station forecourt. Local buses arrive and depart from here as does the Jurassic Breezer open top bus. In bad weather the service still runs but with a closed top bus so you don't have to sit out in the rain. There is a taxi rank at the bottom of the station forecourt. The station forecourt opens on to Kings Road West. Cross the road and turn right at the roundabout onto Station Road to reach the shops and the beach. Swanage has a lot of local independent shops which are well worth a visit.

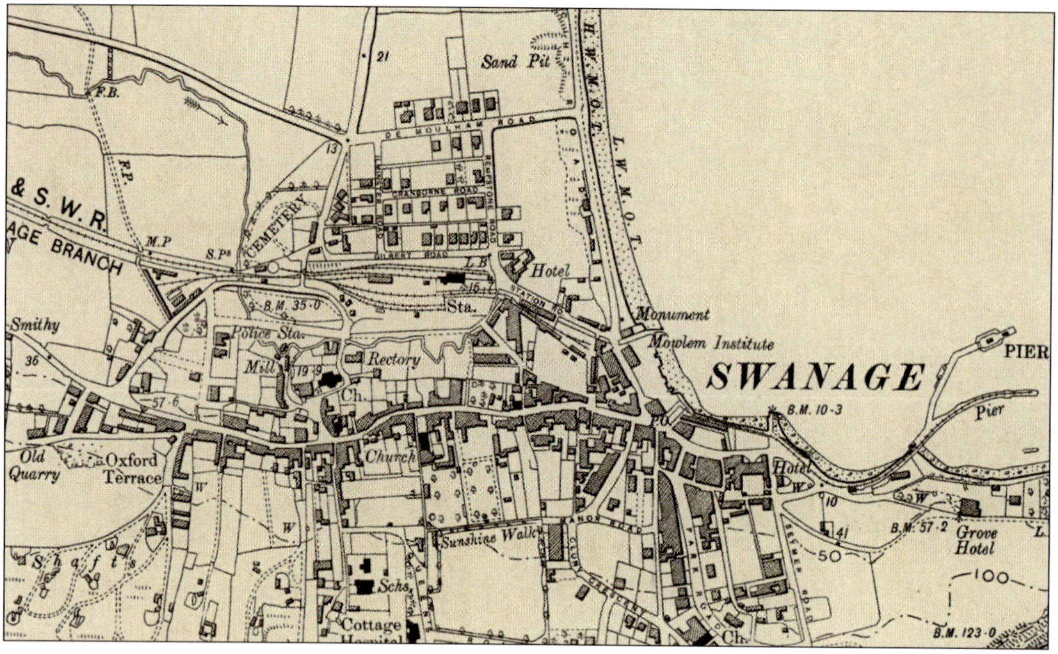


**Swanage in** 1900. The extent of the railway station and yards in the centre of the map. The marked railway line which extends from the yard and down the back of the shops in the Station Road served the stone stores for locally quarried Purbeck stone. The railway marked on the pier is the independent Swanage Pier Tramway. Ordnance Survey, Dorset LVII.SW (includes: Swanage.) - Ordnance Survey Six-inch England and Wales, 1900 (nls.uk). *Reproduced with the permission of the National Library of Scotland*

Heading down Station Road you will reach a junction. Shore Road to the left will take you along Swanage Beachfront from where you can access the award winning sandy 'Blue Flag' beach and the calm waters of Swanage Bay.

If you turn to the right along Institute Road you will pass more shops until you reach a roundabout. The road ahead is the High Street with more retail outlets both to the right and left. Turning left onto The Square after the roundabout you will arrive on the sea front again. To the right at the end of the buildings you will find Swanage Museum and Heritage Centre. The museum is well worth a visit, whilst relatively small it is full of interesting displays about the history and people of Swanage. There are fascinating displays about art and artists who have lived and worked in the Isle of Purbeck, the history and heritage of Swanage, once known as Swanwich, and the Jurassic Coast. The museum also has a well-stocked gift shop selling souvenirs and books related to Dorset and Swanage. It is free to visit but opening hours vary during different times of the year, which are publicised on the museum's website.

Continuing past the museum and turning right along the sea you will reach Swanage Pier. As you walk along the cobbled path you might notice rails embedded in the stones and even a set of points splitting the rails into two paths.

**A view** across Swanage Bay. The long sandy beaches for which the resort is famous can be seen stretching into the distance. *Richard Marks*

These are the remains of the old Swanage Pier Tramway which opened in 1858. The tramway had no connection with the L&SWR Swanage branch and should not be confused with the branch. The narrow gauge rails that remain represent the second tramway, the first was built to the same standard gauge that the main railways were built to in Britain, but it was rebuilt to a narrow gauge before the opening of the public pier. The tramway was used to transport stone from the storage sheds, which were located to the right. The tram was horse drawn, and

**The remains** of Swanage Pier Tramway with the rails set into the stone path. The rails are around the corner of the building occupied by Swanage Museum. This was one end of the tramway; the rails went no further and were never connected to the L&SWR. *Richard Marks*

**The approach** to Swanage Pier from the tramway. c.1880. In the middle distance is the toll booth for the pier. *Swanage Museum*

**Swanage Pier** Tramway c.1880. *Swanage Museum*

transported Purbeck stone from the storage sheds to the old pier where it was loaded onto ships.

Fish was also carried on the tramway to a new fish store built alongside the tramway in 1855. The Swanage Pier Tramway stopped transporting stone once the railway became the main, and more convenient, method of transporting locally quarried stone from the town. It survived in use until the 1930s still carrying fish from the fishing boats using Swanage Harbour. The original timber supports of the Old Pier can still be seen but are now derelict.

Follow the tracks to Swanage Pier. The original pier was built in 1859 for the Swanage Pier and Tramway Company but by 1874 it had become clear that the pier could not cope with the increasing number of day trippers arriving on the steamer service from Poole and Bournemouth. A new pier was needed although construction did not start until 1895, finally opening in 1897. The pier continued to be used until 1940 when the land end was blown up as a precaution against invasion. The section was replaced in 1948.

**Swanage Pier** Tramway c.1880. Whilst slightly damaged, this is one of the handful of Victorian images which survive and so has been included. The toll booth on the right collected entry fees for people who wished to use the pier. There was also a charge for parcels being taken onto the pier. Both tolls were one penny. *Swanage Museum*

**Swanage Pier** in August 2024. *Richard Marks*

The pier is now a grade II listed building due to its historical significance and since 1994 it has been in the care of the Swanage Pier Trust. The pier is well worth a visit both to see the excellent restoration that has been carried out, and to follow in the footsteps of those Victorian and Edwardian holidaymakers who came before. There is a small charge to enter the pier which supports the work of the trust, and opening times vary during the year. On occasion parts may be closed for private functions. Details of prices and opening times as well as a more detailed history can be found on the trust's website.

Whilst exploring Swanage, you will no doubt be quite hungry. There are many good restaurants and pubs in the town serving a wide variety of food and drink. More information about the great restaurants and pubs in Swanage can be found on the Swanage page of the Visit Dorset website.

At the end of your day out, head back to the station and hop on the train back to Norden.

Enjoy your visit to the beautiful Isle of Purbeck and the Swanage Railway.

**Swanage High** Street. *Richard Marks*

# A TRIP ALONG THE LINE

There is a lot to be seen from the window of your train as it heads along Swanage Railway. Let's take a trip from Norden and look out at the Isle of Purbeck. All the references to what can be seen from the train in the tour of the line that follows assume that you are travelling from Norden to Swanage. On the return journey, or if you are setting out from Swanage the sights and scenes will be on the opposite side of the train as you travel.

Walking onto the platform we first pass through a pair of stone abutments which once carried a bridge upon which one of the clay tramways ran. Collecting our tickets at the booking office we proceed onto the platform where our train headed by a gently simmering and hissing steam locomotive awaits. Looking past the train, we catch our first glimpse of the castle in Corfe Castle village, towering over the landscape.

Boarding our train at Norden and settling into our seats we can see the railway's two cranes stored on the siding to the right, although sometimes one of them might be out and about on the railway earning its keep. Both are operational and are used by the railway on civil engineering works and to lift parts of locomotives when needed. With a wave of the guard's flag and a whistle from our engine we set off for Swanage.

As the train leaves the platform, we pass under the bridge which used to carry the Fayle Tramway over the Swanage Branch. Corfe Castle dominates the skyline to the right of the train whilst to our left we can see the pathway that accompanies the railway towards Corfe Castle village. As we continue our journey, we pass the National Trust car park and Corfe Castle visitor centre on the right side of the train. We cross a short viaduct over the B3351 to Studland before the train dives into a short cutting.

***Above*: The ruined** keep at Corfe Castle from within the outer walls. *Richard Marks*

***Opposite*: Visiting from** the Isle of Wight Steam Railway, O2 class number 24 *Calbourne* waits to rejoin its train at Norden having run round. The bridge over the railway once carried the clay tramway, which it may do once more once funds to restore it have been raised. *Richard Marks*

The train emerges from the cutting as we enter Corfe Castle village, on the right we look down on the roofs of the houses below our vantage point of the railway embankment before the landscape climbs back up to join us. Crossing a bridge we enter Corfe Castle station. To the right we can see the original railway station building beautifully restored and maintained by the railway's staff and volunteers. On the left side we have the platform onto which we could alight from the train if we wished but today, Swanage is our destination so we stay in our comfortable seats.

W
24

**The original** signal box at Corfe Castle station. Of note are the unusual small windows in the front of the box. These replaced the more typical large windows usually seen as the signal box faced the first floor rooms of the station master's house in the station building. *John Scott-Morgan Collection.*

The large signal box we can see out of the train on our platform was rebuilt to replace the original demolished by British Railways long before the line closed. Behind the station, a group of buildings makes up the local arts centre, artists' studios and workshops, which we might decide to visit on the way back perhaps. In the distance stretch panoramic views of Purbeck, dominated by Purbeck Ridge. We can see tiny figures of walkers atop the ridge heading towards Swanage or Norden, but today is not a day for being that adventurous. Perhaps another time, walk to Swanage and get the train back? We shall see.

We pause for a moment at Corfe Castle whilst new travellers join us on the train and the signaller exchanges the single line access token with the driver so we can proceed safely to Harman's Cross. The guard blows his whistle and waves his green flag, and with a whistle our steam locomotive pulls us out of the station as our guard hops back aboard.

As the train begins to move, we pass the old goods shed in the yard on the right, which is now the Corfe Castle railway museum, somewhere else to visit on our way back. Next to the goods shed sits the old cattle dock, once used to

**A view** from the Purbeck Ridge walking route across the valley. The Swanage Railway's train to Norden can be seen passing. The walk involves some steep climbs so is for the more advanced hiker. *Rosalind Marks*

send cattle and sheep by rail but now a picnic area. We go under the footbridge linking the two platforms and lastly we pass a railway coach in the yard siding which is the station café, before we see the DMU servicing facility, most likely with the railway's two sets awaiting their next turn of duty. Our train gathers speed and we leave Corfe Castle behind. Looking back from the right of the train we can see stunning views of the castle against the sky which can be seen more clearly coming back from Swanage as we face in the direction of travel.

Looking out of the window we admire the landscape vistas which unfold on both sides of the trains. Those hills were, and some still are, the source of some

**The beginning** of the walk from Corfe Castle to Swanage. Swanage bay and the town can be seen in the far distance. The walk is not for everyone as there are some steep climbs, but it is well worth doing if you can. The views and scenery are stunning. *Rosalind Marks*

of the stone and ball clay which was mined so intensively once, but we see little evidence of the industry now.

We continue under two bridges; the first is a crossing allowing the farmer to get from one part of his farm to another, the second takes us under the A351 main road to Swanage before the scenery opens out once more and we gaze across the unspoilt rural landscapes. As we approach Harman's Cross, the railway runs past some of the campsites which are common around the village. On the right of the train after the last campsite are lines of stored coaches and freight wagons, some are in service but not in use today, but most are waiting for the restorer's touch before they can work again.

We slow to a stop and wait at the signal outside the station. We are crossing with the other service running today and we have to wait for the train from

**L&SWR's T9,** 30120 at Harman's Cross. *Mark Pollard*

Swanage to enter the station and surrender the token for that section before we can continue into the other platform. Looking to the left, on the ground is the green body of an old coach. The coach body is what remains of L&SWR coach No. 911/0695, a six wheeled 3rd class carriage built in 1885 and withdrawn in 1921. Once part of a house it arrived on the railway in 1976 and awaits its turn for restoration. The signal clears and with a whistle we start moving and slowly head into the station, passing the Norden bound train on the right.

Waiting for the single line token which allows us to proceed to be given to the driver and for passengers to alight or join the train, we admire the station gardens and the buildings on the left of the train. Everything we see was created by the railway's volunteers and staff, there once was no station here. With a whistle the other train sets off to Norden and reveals the other half of the station. The lovely station building looks as if it had always been there as do the mature station gardens, clearly tended lovingly by the station's staff. Even the signal box at the Norden end of the station is new, truly a testament to the work and ambition of those who rebuilt the railway we are enjoying, from nothing.

It is our turn to leave, and with a whistle we set off once more for our destination. Leaving the station we head under a road bridge and into a short cutting before emerging once more into the Purbeck countryside. On the right of the train lies another campsite whilst on the left we see some large private houses overlooking the railway and the fields beyond. The train goes over a level crossing which allows a farm access road to cross the railway, to the right in the near distance we can see the farm buildings.

Heading on, the line enters a wood. Trees line both sides of the railway until the train leaves them behind, goes over a farm crossing and we see open countryside on both sides of the train once more. The bridge crossing the line as we head on to Swanage carries the A351, once again crossing the railway. Passing small coppices and fields our train slows as we arrive at Herston Halt in case anyone is waiting on the platform or has asked the guard to let them off there .

**The locomotive** servicing and coaling facility can be seen on the right. *Mark Pollard*

Will we stop? Today, no, nobody is waiting for the train, and we accelerate once more. The landscape changes now as we are coming into the outskirts of Swanage. Passing a trade park on the left and houses on the right we dive under the A351 for the last time. After the bridge the train runs past the bottom of private gardens to our right, a camp site among trees and playing fields on the left.

Suddenly on our right we can see lines of the railway's locomotives some of which are stored out of traffic awaiting their turn in the overhaul workshop, but most are waiting their turn and may be working next time we visit. One may even be in light steam being prepared for tomorrow's trains.

After we pass the lines of engines, on the left we see the old engine shed and turntable. Through the windows of the shed we catch a glimpse of a locomotive but what it is we can't be sure. Sometimes there will be a steam engine on the turntable being readied for another service or maybe tomorrow's trains but today it is empty. Heading under the last bridge on the line we arrive into Swanage station, passing the old goods shed on the right, and our journey is over, for now.

# THE LOCOMOTIVE FLEET

The Swanage Railway has a particularly interesting fleet of locomotives. Whilst there is a large fleet, many of them will not be in steam at the time of your visit. Steam locomotives need to be taken out of use at least every ten years for a full overhaul and renewal of the boiler so that a new boiler certificate can be issued allowing it to be steamed for a further period. Sometimes an engine might be away visiting another heritage railway or may not be available for technical reasons and may be undergoing maintenance, although it may well be visible in the locomotive yard at Swanage. There will be occasions when there is an opportunity to see an engine which is not normally resident on the line. Locomotives visiting for a gala weekend may sometimes stay for longer and operate normal services on the Swanage branch.

These extended stays are publicised in the news pages on the railway's website.

Some locomotives, particularly the Victorian engines, are used less frequently due to their age.

The following is intended only to give you a feel for the locomotives you might see at work on the line. If you are intending to visit to see one particular locomotive, then it is advisable to check the railways planned roster to see which dates the engine may be running.

## The Steam Fleet

The steam locomotive fleet is made up of different types of engine, mostly associated with British Rail's Southern Region, the Southern Railway and its predecessors which owned and operated the Swanage branch line.

Some of the railway's fleet are Oliver Bullied-designed Pacifics. The arrangement of four carrying wheels on a bogie at the front, six large driving wheels, and two carrying wheels on the rear truck (4-6-2) is referred as a 'pacific' in railway terminology.

The locomotives are three different types which can be seen in original rebuilt or un-rebuilt form. All of the Bulleids were originally built in 'air smoothed' form with a casing around the boiler designed to reduce drag. The flat sides of the casing led to the locomotives being known as 'Spam Cans'. The engines were usually used to haul long distance express passenger trains, although they could also be found on fast freight trains and 'semi-fast' limited stop passenger trains.

Many of the locomotives, but not all, were rebuilt by British Railways into a more conventional form, also doing away with some of the more advanced but troublesome features of the original design. Many of these locomotives have been preserved, some which are resident on the Swanage Railway.

The Swanage Railway is home to both original and rebuilt examples of two of the classes. The larger 'Merchant Navy' class which came first and were named after ocean shipping lines does not have an example at Swanage, although some can occasionally be seen visiting the line, and one, owned by Southern Locomotives Limited, was undergoing the early stages of restoration in 2024 so may appear at some point but maybe not for a while.

## 34028 *Eddystone*

34028 is a 'West Country' class, all of which were named after places in the west of England. This class is identical in every way to the Battle of Britain class, the split being more for convenience due to the number of locomotives in the classes, 110 built in total, and the naming conventions used for each. 34028 is named after the lighthouse on Eddystone Rocks which lie just off the coast of Cornwall, nine miles southwest of Rame Head. The rocks, strangely, fall within the city limits of Plymouth and so are technically in Devon.

*Eddystone* was built in 1946 in the same form as both *Manston* and *257 Squadron*. The locomotive was rebuilt by British Railways in 1959 into the more conventional form in which it can be seen today. 34028 was withdrawn by British Railways after just six years, in 1965 and sent to Barry Scrapyard where it languished until 1986 when it was purchased by the Southern Pacific Rescue Group, which later merged with Southern Locomotives Limited. The engine was slowly restored by its owners and entered service on the Swanage Railway in 2003. Withdrawn from traffic in 2014, *Eddystone* returned to traffic in 2021.

**Rebuilt West** Country Class, 34028 *Eddystone* at Corfe Castle with a Swanage bound train. *Richard Marks*

## 34053 *Sir Keith Park*

34053 is a rebuilt version of the 'Battle of Britain' class of locomotives. The locomotive is named after Air Chief Marshal Sir Keith Park, the commander of the Royal Air Force's 11 Group which was responsible for the air defence of the southeast of Great Britain during the Second World War and faced the brunt of the assault on the country during the Battle of Britain.

34053 was originally built in air smoothed form in 1947 and was rebuilt by British Railways in 1960. It was withdrawn from service in 1965 and sent, like so many other redundant steam locomotives, to Barry Scrapyard. The locomotive remained in the sea air at Barry until 1984, although it was purchased, in 1979. Restoration progressed slowly and the engine passed from one owner to another until it was eventually purchased by Southern Locomotives Limited. *Sir Keith Park* was restored, its return to steam taking twelve years. Initially based at the Severn Valley Railway, the engine returned to Swanage in 2018.

**Battle of** Britain Class, 34053 *Sir Keith Park* at Swanage. The locomotive is being prepared for duty at the railway's 'Strictly Bulleid II' gathering of eight Bulleid Pacifics. *Mark Pollard*

The locomotive moved to the Spa Valley Railway in 2020 after a period out of traffic for repair. Withdrawn for overhaul in 2022, the locomotive returned to steam in 2024 and was present at the Swanage Railway's 'Strictly Bullied' gala. *Sir Keith* returned to the Spa Valley Railway after the gala, but as part of the Southern Locomotives Limited collection may well be seen on the Swanage Railway at times.

## 34070 *Manston*

34070 is a 'Battle of Britain' class locomotive and like *257 Squadron* is in the original form as first built. The engine is named after the Royal Air Force

**Unrebuilt West** Country Class, 34070 *Manston* arriving at Harman's Cross during a rain shower. The locomotive has deliberately been allowed to become heavily weathered to represent how many steam locomotives looked during the latter days of steam on British Railways. *Richard Marks*

station on the south-east tip of Kent, which was an important airfield in the defence of Britain. The airfield was, due to its location, in the frontline during the Battle of Britain, and was often bombed. Later in the Second World War it was used as the base for the testing of Barnes Wallis's famous 'bouncing bomb' used in the Dambusters raid. The airfield was an important point from which gliders carrying troops and equipment departed during the airborne attack on Arnhem in 1944, as well as being the airfield from which the Royal Air Force's first operational jet fighter squadron operated with Gloster Meteor aircraft during 1944.

34070 was built in 1947 and was withdrawn by British Railways in 1964. It was purchased by the Manston Locomotive Preservation Society, which later merged with Southern Locomotives Limited who still own the locomotive today. *Manston* was restored and entered service at the Swanage Railway in 2008. It was withdrawn for overhaul in 2017 and returned to service in 2021.

## 34072 *257 Squadron*

34072 is a 'Battle of Britain' Class locomotive in its original air smoothed form. The class was all named after airfields, Royal Air Force squadrons, aircraft and people involved in the Battle of Britain. This engine is named after the Royal Air Force's 257 Squadron which flew Hawker Hurricane fighters from RAF Northolt during the battle.

The locomotive was built in 1948 and withdrawn from service by British Railways in 1964. 34072 was purchased by Southern Locomotives Limited from Barry Scrapyard and restored in 1990. It moved to Swanage in 1992 and ran there until being withdrawn for overhaul in 2003. The locomotive returned to service on the railway in 2018 following a major overhaul.

**Battle of** Britain Class, 34072 *257 Squadron* arriving at Harman's Cross with a Swanage bound train. *Mark Pollard*

## 34010 *Sidmouth*

30410 is a 'West Country' class locomotive which, like *Eddystone* was rebuilt by British Railways. First built in air smoothed form by the Southern Railway in 1945 at Brighton Works, *Sidmouth* was rebuilt in 1959. 34010 is named after the town on the south coast of Devon, located just fourteen miles southeast of Exeter.

The locomotive was withdrawn in 1965 during the final culls of steam on the national network, and was sent to Barry Scrapyard. There it stayed until 1982, when it was purchased and moved to the North Yorkshire Moors Railway. The planned restoration in Yorkshire did not proceed due to a lack of resources, the locomotive eventually being acquired by Southern Locomotives Limited in 1997. Restoration started and has slowly progressed since. In 2024 *Sidmouth* is still under restoration, but will return to steam. It is likely that 34010 will be seen once more hauling trains, and probably on the Swanage Railway.

## 80104 British Railways Standard Class '4MT'

80104 is one of 15 surviving members of a class of 155 locomotives designed and built by British Railways in the 1950s. The class have no tender, the coal being kept in a bunker immediately behind the cab, with water being stored in the tanks alongside each side of the boiler immediately in front of the cab. The self-contained arrangement of the engines meant that, like similar engines of other types, they were referred to as 'tank engines'. The locomotives were designed for use primarily on commuter and outer suburban trains; however, they could be found performing a variety of other tasks, including heavier branch line trains and local freights. The design was able to run as effectively in reverse as it was forward, which made them extremely useful and flexible. The combination of economy, flexibility and power makes the class ideal for heritage railways.

80104 was built in 1955 and was used mainly on the London, Tilbury and Southend line out of Fenchurch Street terminus in London, before being transferred to Wales in 1962. The engine was withdrawn by British Railways in 1965 and like all but one of the other preserved members of the class was sent to Barry Scrapyard. It was purchased by the Southern Steam Trust in 1984, cosmetically restored and placed on display at Swanage railway station. The engine was moved to part of the old railway works at Swindon for restoration. Southern Locomotives Limited, then the owners of 80104, were asked to vacate the site when the works were closed and scheduled for redevelopment. As a result, the locomotive returned again to Swanage for

**Standard Class** 4 80104, September 2023. *Ian Kirk*

completion of its restoration under a new agreement made with the Swanage Railway after the opening of the railway's new engineering workshops. Returning to steam in 1995, the locomotive joined the operating fleet at Swanage, where it proved a useful addition. 80104 returned to traffic once more in 2006 following withdrawal for overhaul in 2005 and continued to work until 2021 when it was withdrawn for overhaul once more. The engine was due to re-enter service in 2025.

## The Southern 'Moguls'

The railway is home to a trio of Southern Railway 'mogul' locomotives as well as the Bulleid fleet. The term 'mogul' refers to the wheel arrangement of two guiding wheels at the front on a moving pony truck, and six coupled driving wheels (2-6-0). The wheel arrangement was one of the preferred design standards on Britain's railways, although less common than the 4-6-0 wheel arrangement. The arrangement was used for mixed traffic locomotives, which were designed to be as capable on freight as they were on passenger trains. The engines of this design were mid power range but nonetheless very capable. The size and power of these locomotives makes them perfect for Britain's heritage railways as they are able to haul any train the railway is likely to operate whilst being economic on coal use.

## 31625 Southern Railway 'U' Class

31625 (1625 prior to the nationalisation of Britain's railways in 1948) was one of the batch of new 'U' class locomotives built by the Southern Railway to the same design as the rebuilt River Class version. Built in 1929 at Ashford Works in Kent, the locomotive is identical to its sister 31806. Withdrawn from service by British Rail in 1964, 31625 languished in Barry scrapyard until 1980 when it was purchased privately for use on the Mid-Hants Railway. The engine was returned to steam and ran there for some time. Following an overhaul to mainline standard, 31625 was a popular performer on railway excursions. The locomotive was withdrawn needing major repairs to the firebox and boiler and stored awaiting its turn in the workshops.

**U Class** 31625, stored waiting for funds to allow restoration, seen at Corfe Castle station, 2016. *Alan Wilson*

The locomotive moved to the Swanage Railway in 2014 with 31806 and 31874. It has not yet run at Swanage and was stored awaiting its turn in the overhaul queue in 2024.

## 31806 Southern Railway 'U' Class

31806 (1806 before the nationalisation of Britain's railways in 1948) is one of four surviving Southern Railway 'U' Class mixed traffic locomotives. The class consisted of fifty locomotives of which thirty were new builds and twenty were rebuilds of 'K' Class tank engines. The 'K' Class, designed by Richard Maunsell, were built for the South Eastern and Chatham Railway's express services and was mechanically similar to the company's 'N' Class tender engines. The 'K' class were built in 1925 and 1926 and given names of rivers, becoming known as the 'River Class'. The locomotives were found to be unstable at speed, partly due to the poor condition of the South Eastern and Chatham Railway's main line. They became known by crews as 'Rolling Rivers' because of this tendency caused by surging of water in the side tanks. One of the class was involved in

**U Class** 31806 at Norden. *Mark Pollard*

the Sevenoaks railway accident in 1927 and as a result the decision was taken to rebuild them as tender engines.

The rebuilt engines looked almost identical to Maunsell's 'N' Class and were as capable and useful. 31806, formerly A806 *River Torridge*, is one of those locomotives that were rebuilt, and is the only survivor of that group. Leaving Brighton Works in 1928 the locomotive served until withdrawn by British Railways in 1964 when it was sent to Barry Scrapyard. Purchased privately in 1976 for restoration on the Mid-Hants Railway, the locomotive was the 85th to leave Barry. Restoration started in 1979, and 31806 returned to steam in 1981.

The locomotive arrived at Swanage, its new home, in 2014 and entered service. It became popular with crews and was in demand for galas on other railways until its boiler certificate, which allows it to be steamed, expired at the end of its ten years in 2021. The locomotive was undergoing an overhaul in 2024 with the hope of returning this useful locomotive to service as soon as possible.

## 31874 Southern Railway 'N' Class

31874 is the sole surviving member of a class of 80 mixed traffic locomotives designed for the South Eastern and Chatham Railway by their chief mechanical engineer Richard Maunsell.

The first of the class was built in 1917, and found to be so useful that the design continued to be built by the Southern Railway of which the South Eastern became part in the railway grouping of 1923. In order to provide work for engineering workshops after the end of the First World War, fifty N Class locomotives were built from kits of parts supplied to the Royal Arsenal at Woolwich. The class thus became known as 'Woolworths' after the now defunct high street store which stocked a wide variety of useful items which could be used across the home and garden. 31874 is also the only surviving locomotive built at Woolwich and is thus an important historical artefact.

The engines could be found on a wide variety of workings, being powerful and reliable. The qualities of the design make 31874 the ideal type of locomotive for a heritage railway, being economic on coal and able to handle even the heaviest and most intensive services on the line with ease.

31874 was built in 1925 at Ashford Works in Kent and withdrawn by British Railways (after receiving a 3 prefix to its original number 1874 at nationalisation in 1948) from Exmouth Junction Shed in 1964. The engine was purchased for scrap by Dai Woodham and was sent to his scrapyard at Barry. It remained there until 1974, when it was purchased privately for use on the Mid-Hants Railway in Hampshire. Returning to steam in 1977 the engine was operational when the first part of the old railway line was reopened as a heritage railway. Issues with the firebox which needed complete replacement meant that the engine was withdrawn in 1998. 31874 moved to Swanage in 2014 and work to overhaul the locomotive began. It is hoped that the locomotive will be seen again in operation in the not-too-distant future.

## The South Western Fleet

The Swanage Railway is home to a very rare collection of Victorian locomotives all of which were built by the L&SWR during the nineteenth century. The Swanage branch is an ideal home for the engines since the railway was originally part of the L&SWR network, and an important line both for freight and holiday makers.

The South Western Fleet consists of three rare Victorian locomotives, all of which were built by the L&SWR, the original builders of the Swanage railway. Two of the collection are unique, the other being only one of two that survived into preservation and the only one that is likely to ever steam.

## 563 London and South Western Railway 'T3' Class

563 is a beautiful example of Victorian engineering and proof of the engineer's maxim that 'if it looks right, it is right'.

The T3 class numbered just twenty, although this was quite normal for the time, many railway companies constructing a wide variety of locomotives for a specific purpose. The first T3 entered service with the L&SWR in 1892 and was built at their Nine Elms workshops in London. The last of the twenty arrived in 1893. The Victorian engineer's expertise and attention to detail, coupled with the desire to make machines 'look right' resulted in elegant designs. The T3 survives as a testament to British engineering excellence.

All of the class passed to the Southern Railway at the grouping of railway companies in 1923 when the 120 different British railway companies were amalgamated into just four large regional companies, the Big Four. Replaced by more modern traction, the first withdrawals began in 1930 and by the end of 1933 only three remained. The last two, 571 and 563, were kept in traffic due to the start of the Second World War when every engine was desperately needed. Number 571, worn out and in need of repair, was withdrawn in 1944, but 563 soldiered

**An immaculate** looking steam locomotive that took 6 years to be fully overhauled and returned to service at the Swanage Railway in October 2023, the LSWR T3 Class 563 locomotive pulls an afternoon train up from Swanage Station past the main yard with SR U Class 31806 sitting in the yard receiving some work. *B. Ward*

on until it was withdrawn in 1945 and set aside for preservation. The locomotive was cosmetically restored for the celebrations marking the centenary of Waterloo station in 1948, after which it passed into the National Collection, and until 2011 could be seen in the National Railway Museum at Clapham and then at York when the museum moved there. In 2011 the engine was sent to Canada to star in a theatrical production of *The Railway Children,* a role it reprised at King's Cross between 2014 and 2017.

After the end of the play's run, the locomotive, viewed as being a 'duplicate' of other similar locomotives, was transferred into the care of the Swanage Railway Trust. The trust now owned the locomotive. The railway announced their intention to restore the engine, and following a successful public appeal and a positive evaluation of the locomotive, restoration began. 563 returned to service in late 2023 and can be seen working services on the railway. The opportunity to see a Victorian express locomotive doing what it was designed for is a sight not to be missed.

**L&SWR T3** class just after arrival from the National Railway Museum and before restoration. The locomotive was temporarily placed on display in the cattle dock at Corfe Castle whilst funds were being raised for its overhaul. The faded paint which the engine wore when it arrived makes an interesting comparison with the striking paintwork the restorers produced. *Richard Marks*

The locomotive only runs on selected days and it is advised that you refer to the locomotive roster publicised on the Swanage Railway website. The roster lists the locomotives that the railway plans to have in operation on those days but due to operational necessity and maintenance of what are now elderly machines, the railway may have to substitute other steam locomotives at short notice on any given day.

## 30053 London and South Western Railway 'M7' Class

30053 (53 prior to the nationalisation of Britain's railways in 1948) is an M7 class tank locomotive. The engine was built by the L&SWR in 1905 as part of a class of 105 locomotives. The M7s were designed to replace older and less

**L&SWR M7,** 30053 at Swanage running round the train before heading back to Norden. The M7 is in Southern Railway livery wearing the number 53. The British Railway's number 30053 can just be seen under the number on the bunker. The resident Class 121 diesel unit can be seen on the head shunt behind the locomotive. *Richard Marks*

powerful tank engines on the intensive passenger services on the South London network operated by the L&SWR. The first locomotive left Eastleigh works in 1897. The class were not limited to the suburban services and could be found on semi-fast services between London to Portsmouth and even as far as Exeter and Plymouth.

As services out of Waterloo became heavier and more powerful locomotives capable of longer distance journeys became available, the class began to be cascaded to other services on which they proved more than capable. The electrification of the suburban network under the L&SWR from 1915 saw the engines being used on services to Guildford and Reading. Continued electrification under the Southern Railway after 1924 saw the locomotives being made redundant on these lines, but they proved extremely capable of working services on branch lines and rural routes where they excelled. The members of the class allocated to Bournemouth shed could be found working services on the Swanage branch until the very last M7s were withdrawn by British Rail in the 1960s.

30053 is one of only two locomotives which survive, the other (30245) is in the National Collection and can be found at the National Railway Museum in York. 30053 is the only one of the pair ever likely to steam. The engine was sold to Steamtown in Bellows Falls, Vermont in the United States of America in 1967 where it remained until 1987 when it was purchased and returned to Britain. Owned by Drummond Locomotives Limited (named after the designer of the class, Dugald Drummond), 30053 is based at an appropriate home on the Swanage Railway. The engine arrived in 1987 and required a five year overhaul to return it to service. Since 1992 the engine has proved a popular and reliable member of the railway's fleet of steam locomotives. It is both powerful and economical on coal, making it ideal for the heritage services operated by the railway.

The engine was withdrawn from service in 2019 for an overhaul which was, like so much else, delayed by the Covid Pandemic of 2020. The locomotive remains out of traffic in 2024, but it likely that the last operational survivor of the class will return to steam once more in the near future.

## 30120 London and South Western Railway 'T9' Class

30120 (120 prior to the nationalisation of Britain's railways in 1948) is the last survivor of the L&SWR T9 Class of sixty-six engines. The locomotives were designed by Dugald Drummond, the L&SWR chief engineer, for express passenger services in the west of England. Introduced into service in 1899, the T9s were probably the finest examples of Victorian railway engineering excellence. Thirty-five locomotives were built at the company's Eastleigh works, the remainder by Dübs & Co of Glasgow. The engines proved extremely capable, and with excellent acceleration and a high speed of up to 85mph, they became known as 'greyhounds'.

They served the railway well, passing into the ownership of British Railways after nationalisation in 1948. The class worked until the last example, 30120, was withdrawn in 1961. The engine was earmarked by British Railways Board for retention as part of the national collection as it was such an important part of

**L&SWR Drummond** Class T9 4-4-0 No.30120 in British Railways lined black livery approaching Corfe Castle on the 12.00 Swanage - River Frome service, during the Swanage Railway Autumn Steam Gala, 11 October 2019. *Hugh Llewelyn*

the history of Britain's railways. The locomotive did not immediately pass into a museum though. It was taken out of traffic and sent to Eastleigh for an overhaul, during which time it was repainted into its original L&SWR green. 30120 then returned to working ordinary services as well as special trains until it was finally withdrawn by British Rail and passed into the national collection. Stored until the early 1980s the engine was loaned to the Mid-Hants Railway where it was restored and returned to steam. It moved on to the Swanage Railway in 1991 where it ran until the expiry of its boiler certificate in 1993. 30120 then moved to the Bluebell Railway where it was stored under cover but on display for visitors to admire.

The engine returned to steam in 2010 at the Bodmin and Wenford Railway in Cornwall following a major overhaul. It worked on the line in Cornwall, but also visited other railways including Swanage. In 2017, repairs were required which were undertaken by the Swanage Railway, after which the locomotive remained in Dorset, working services from Swanage. Remaining on loan from the National Railway Museum, 30120 continued to work services until the expiry of its boiler certificate in 2020. 30120 was then placed in store awaiting overhaul but it is hoped that it will return to service before the expiry of 563's boiler certificate so it can work alongside its sister once more.

### The Diesel Fleet

The Swanage Railway is home to a small collection of diesel locomotives and multiple units, all of which have long since been replaced by more modern traction on Britain's national network. Whilst not having the romance of a steam locomotive, the diesel fleet on the railway is no less important in telling the story of the history of the railways. It is possible that the diesel locomotives may be carrying either their later number with the class prefix followed by the individual engine number (for example 33 012, is number 12 of the class 33 locomotives) or with their original number allocated when steam was still prominent. In order to distinguish between types of locomotive, British Railways added a D prefix to the number of diesel and an E prefix to the number of electric locomotives. The original number is presented in brackets below.

### 33012 (D6515) and 33111 (D6528) British Rail Class '33' Crompton

33012 and 33111 are both members of a class of diesel electric locomotive once a common sight on the railways in the south of England. The ninety-eight locomotives of class 33 were built between 1960 and 1962 by Birmingham Railway Carriage and Wagon Company located in Smethwick. The company was formed in 1854 and was one of the major constructors of railway locomotives for Britain's railways as well as aeroplanes, tanks and buses. British Railways subcontracted the construction of the class 33s to the Birmingham company since their own workshops were busy constructing steam locomotives and other classes of diesels and electrics. The class 33s were built with Crompton Parkinson electrical equipment and so became known as 'Cromptons'.

The locomotives were built for the Southern Region of British Rail, based upon the Type 2 design (later known as class 26) built for Scottish Region. The engine is a Sulzer diesel engine which was built by Vickers-Armstrong at Barrow-in-Furness. In railway terminology, the term BO refers to two powered axles per bogie, whilst CO refers to three powered axles on a bogie. The axles on each bogie of a class 33 are powered and thus they are referred to as BO-BOs.

The resulting locomotives were powerful and capable additions to the Southern Region locomotive fleet. The engines were often to be found working through Wareham to Weymouth and also on the Swanage branch. Twenty-nine of the class have been preserved and have proved to be ideal for heritage railway services.

33012 (D6515) was delivered to British Rail in 1960, withdrawn in 1997 and is now owned by the 71A Locomotive Group. The group was founded in 1996 by a group of Eastleigh-based train drivers to preserve a class 33. The locomotive was purchased from EWS in 1997 and restored, arriving at the Swanage Railway in 1999. The locomotive was named *Lt Jenny Lewis RN* in 2014 in memory of the helicopter observer in the Royal Navy who was killed along with the pilot Lieutenant Rod Skidmore when their Lynx helicopter crashed into the sea following major engine failure in 2002. Jenny was a fan of the class 33s and so it was thought to be a fitting memorial to name the locomotive in her honour.

33111 (D6528) was delivered to British Rail in 1960 and was withdrawn in 1991. Purchased by the Class 33/1 Preservation Company Limited, who also

**Class 33** 'Crompton' D6515 (33012) *Lt Jenny Lewis RN* running around its train at Swanage. The locomotive was named in preservation to commemorate Lt Jenny Lewis who died in a Royal Navy helicopter accident. *Richard Marks*

**Class 33** 'Crompton', 33 111 parked in the head shunt at Swanage station awaiting its next turn of duty. *Richard Marks*

own 33108 (D6521), in 1992, the locomotive was completely rebuilt. Following a fifteen-year restoration which involved completely rebuilding the power unit, a full rewire and a full overhaul of the locomotive's bodywork 33108 arrived at Swanage in 2008 and has been in service more or less ever since.

## 08436 (D3551) and 08476 (D3591) British Rail Class '08' Diesel Shunter

The two locomotives are both members of a class of 996 locomotives built by British Railways to replace aging steam locomotives in shunting work.

The class was built between 1953 and 1962, and many of the surviving locomotives are older than some of the steam locomotives preserved on Britain's heritage lines. Once useful locomotives for shunting coaches for trains, and wagons of freight in yards, they became redundant as the nature of trains on Britain's railways changed. The modern multiple unit trains do not need shunting, as with a cab at each end they are able to reverse direction when required, without the need for a shunter to release the train locomotive at terminuses. Only a few of the class are still active on the national network, usually in depots and workshops where units are split for maintenance.

The low maintenance requirement and reliability of the class has meant they have become valuable additions to almost every heritage railway's fleet of locomotives. The nature of the trains run on preserved railway lines means that the work the class 08 was designed for is very much still in demand. There are eighty-seven examples of the class in preservation since they are so useful. 08436 can occasionally be seen carrying its first number D3551, whilst 08476 usually runs with its original number D3591.

## W55028 British Rail Class '121' Bubble Car

W55028 is a single car class '121' diesel railcar with a driving cab at each end. The sixteen single cars were classified as Driving Motor Brake Second (DMBS) in British Rail terminology since they only had second class (referred to more recently as Standard Class) accommodation. In order to increase capacity on busier services, ten single ended trailer vehicles (unpowered) were built which could be coupled to a Class 121. The class 121 became known as a 'Bubble Car' by enthusiasts due to the vague similarity to small cars of the 1960s of the same name. The name has stuck, being used by the type's last mainline operator, Chiltern Railways. The last of the class were

**The Swanage** Railway's Class 121 'Bubble Car' at Swanage. It is coupled to one of the railway's Class 117 diesel multiple units. *Richard Marks*

finally withdrawn in 2017, making them the most long lived of the early DMUs after a service life of 57 years.

The class was designed for use on the lightly used branch lines of the Western Region of British Rail in Cornwall and the Thames Valley, as well as the Bridport branch in Dorset (closed in 1975) and the Severn Beach branch in Bristol. Despite their intended use, class 121 cars could sometimes be found coupled to other DMUs to provide extra capacity on trains between Reading and London Paddington and other services in the Thames Valley.

The class has proved extremely popular with heritage railways. The units are ideal for lightly used services during low season, and for operating shuttles on event weekends. The large windows and view through the leading cab from behind the driver as well as through the trailing cab provide panoramic vistas of the scenery through which your train is passing. A train ride on one of these vehicles can be a fun diversion.

Twelve have been preserved of which one, W55028, can be found on the Swanage Railway. The 'W' prefix refers to the Western Region of British Rail, all DMU and coaching stock used on the region being prefixed in that manner. W55028 arrived on the railway in 2009.

## British Rail Class '117' Diesel Multiple Unit

The Class '117' DMU will be familiar to many commuters as they were used by British Rail's Western Region on the majority of commuter and suburban services in the Thames Valley. All of the sets consisted of three car units made up of a DMBS, Trailer Composite with Lavatory (TCL) and Driving Motor Second (DMS) in a fixed formation. Occasionally a Class '121' single car unit was coupled to one end of the Class '117' set to provide additional seats. The Class '121' and Class '117' were both fitted with equipment which allowed the entire train to be controlled from the cabs at each end of the extended consist making them extremely flexible. All of the Class '117' units were based either at Southall or Reading depots for the operation of Thames Valley services between London Paddington, Reading, Oxford, Newbury and Bedwyn as well as the Windsor, Henley and Marlow branches.

The trains were built by the Pressed Steel Company Limited at their factory in Linwood, Renfrewshire, Scotland on behalf of British Rail. A total of 123 cars of the three types were made and delivered as 39 three car sets plus three spare motor coaches to allow for maintenance.

The units were replaced on services from Paddington after 1992 by the new Class 165 'Network Turbo' trains. Some Class 117s continued in service operating trains from Penzance to Looe until 1997, and some routes from Edinburgh until 1998. The few remaining sets were displaced from Silverlink services in 2000.

The Swanage Railway has two resident class '117' DMUs. One set (DMBS 51356, TCL 59492 and DMS 51392) is often used on the railway's diesel timetable and evening shuttles. The second set (DMBS 51346, TCL 59486 and DMS 51388) is also used on the railway's diesel rota but has also been restored to mainline standards and registered accordingly. The DMBS 51356 was also restored to mainline standard to act as a spare unit for the second set. The intention was to use the second set on shuttles from Norden along the remainder of the branch line to Wareham via Worgret junction.

These services have been suspended following the end of the two year trial due to cost. In 2024 the two Class 117 sets are restricted to the Swanage Railway services between Norden and Swanage, but if funding becomes available to make the service viable, the second set may well run services to Wareham once more in the future.

**Class 121** and Class 117 diesel multiple units pass T9 30120 in the shed at Swanage on one of the Swanage Railway's trial services to Wareham on 30 August 2023. *The Basingstoker*

# HERITAGE CARRIAGES

The Swanage Railway has a large collection of passenger carriages. The majority of the coaches are British Railways standard mark I passenger carriages. All were built by British Railways in their own workshops between 1951 and 1963. The new carriages were designed to replace the older, disparate designs with a fleet of standard stock. This made maintenance easier, and the stock of spares more economic to manage. The coaches were made redundant during the 1970s and into the 1980s as they were replaced by more modern carriages built by British Rail Engineering Limited on behalf of British Rail. Many of the coaches being disposed of by the railway provided a bonus to Britain's new heritage railways who bought large numbers of them from British Rail relatively cheaply. The mark I coach is the mainstay of the Britain's heritage railways.

Some of the carriages in the Swanage Railway's collection are particularly noteworthy, though. Whilst some are awaiting restoration from derelict condition before they can carry passengers once more, others have been restored for us to enjoy once again. The vintage coaches provide us with the opportunity to experience how people travelled by train during the 1930s and even before. Many of the surviving carriages are particularly important and rare examples of Britain's railway heritage. It takes many hours of painstaking restoration work to return a single passenger coach to the rails. The attention to detail required to return a coach to its former glory is impressive. The recreation of the upholstery of the seats, the wooden panelling and lighting inside as well as the painting, signwriting and lining out on the outside are all examples of the work of masters of the craft. The mechanical restoration of a coach is no less an example of expert workmanship. When you are travelling on your day out, spare a thought for the unsung heroes of Britain's heritage railways, the volunteers and staff who work in the carriage workshops.

**Visting from** the Mid-Hants Railway (The Watercress Line) Ivatt Class 2 tank number 41312 runs around its train at Norden. The small concrete hut is a typical Southern Railway lineside 'bothy'. Behind the engine is the grounded body of a vintage coach awaiting restoration. *Richard Marks*

The carriages are often overlooked as important items of historic heritage and sit in the shadows behind the popular steam locomotive. The coaches which are used, or are awaiting restoration, are no less important, and without them you would not be able to enjoy a pleasant day out on any of Britain's heritage railways.

The railway has some vintage L&SWR coaches which are awaiting restoration as well as those which have been or are being restored. Some of these can be seen from the train as you journey down the line. Perhaps you might be able to enjoy travelling on a train of these Edwardian coaches hauled by a locomotive of the same vintage soon. It would be quite an experience.

# SPECIAL EVENTS AND EXPERIENCES

The Swanage Railway runs special events throughout the year in addition to their normal timetabled train service. These vary greatly from large events with visiting locomotives from other railways from across Britain as well as locomotives such as *Flying Scotsman* from the National Collection at the Railway Museum in York, to themed events and celebrations of historical anniversaries.

The railway also offers wonderful experiences which make perfect gifts, even for yourself. The dates of these events vary throughout the year and change over time. To give a flavour of the events which the railway runs some of them are outlined below. Although a proportion of the events were related to particular events in history and may not run again for some time, events on similar themes are not uncommon and so these are included to give you a flavour of the kinds of events that you might like. Not all of these may run each year whilst others such as the Paddle Steamer trips are subject to availability of the ship and the weather.

To give you a flavour of the special trains and events which the railway runs the following are all events which ran in 2024. Most of them are repeated throughout the year, although the gala events, whilst running each year, will vary in theme. Dates will change and new events are often added to the programme of interesting days out and celebrations, so do check the railway's website regularly, you might just find something special.

When considering any experience or event on the Swanage Railway, this guide does not necessarily contain the current offering, and requirements for footplate trips and so on. You should refer to the railway's website to confirm dates, prices and information about the event prior to booking. It is also possible on rare occasions that, for operational reasons, a diesel locomotive may have to be substituted for a steam engine on a given day.

## Devon Belle Observation Car

The Devon Belle was a luxury long distance express train which ran between 1947 and 1954 from London's Waterloo station to Plymouth and Ilfracombe. The train was made up entirely of Pullman coaches which set a new standard of comfort and luxury on the railways. The east and westbound trains departed at 12:00 noon and with few stops en route the journey time was just five and a half hours. The trains had two notable features for the time. All of the seats on the train were bookable, unusual on the railway, and more importantly each train contained a distinctive observation coach at the rear. The two coaches built purely for this service were unusual in having large panoramic windows which gave an unparalleled view of the scenery as the train ran to its destination. When British Railways ceased running the Devon Belle, both coaches were sent to Scotland where they were used on special trains.

Fortunately, when British Railways ceased running the trains the two observation cars, numbers 13 and 14 were sold to preservationists. Number

**The Pullman** observation car at the rear of a Swanage bound train about to depart from Corfe Castle station during a summer rain shower. The large windows give panoramic views of the Purbeck countryside, whilst those at the end of the train give a unique view of the locomotive when travelling in the Swanage direction. *Richard Marks*

14 was sent to the United States with *Flying Scotsman* for a tour of America but spent a period of time as part of an office building in San Fransisco following financial issues during the tour which meant it could not be shipped home. The building became empty and the owner sold the coach to a new group of preservationists and it was repatriated to the Swanage Railway and restored, although the new bar added for the American tour was retained.

The coach is now often used on service trains on the railway where, for a small supplementary fare, you can experience Pullman luxury for a return trip on the line. As the train runs from Swanage to Norden you will be able to take in stunning panoramic views of the Isle of Purbeck and the ruins of Corfe Castle through the large unobstructed windows of the carriage. In the other direction you will be able to see the locomotive working through the end windows of the coach as it will be coupled to the train directly in front of the observation car.

It is worth paying the small supplementary fare, which is run on a first come basis, to enjoy the scenery and the engine. Be aware that seats in the coach are limited and on busy days might be fully occupied. The coach is part of the consist of the train on the days on which it is in use, so will be running all day, so why not have a look round Swanage or Corfe Castle and catch the next train?

The coach is not used on every day that trains run and will not be available on days when the Champagne Afternoon Tea service is being run apart from those who have booked in advance for the afternoon tea. Days when other special events are running may also result in the coach being unavailable. Signs on the platforms at Norden and Swanage make it clear whether the observation coach is available, or just approach one of the railway's friendly platform volunteers and ask.

## Paddle Steamer *Waverley*

The paddle steamer *Waverley*, the world's last paddle steamer still operating at the time of writing, visits Swanage at various times during the year, providing short cruises along the south coast. A variety of options are available such as a paddle steamer cruise from Poole to Swanage (one way), or Swanage to Ryde in the Isle of Wight and return, or from Swanage to cruise along the Jurassic Coast. A combination of a trip on the Swanage Railway and a cruise on the paddle steamer makes for the ultimate steam powered day out.

The steamer does not operate from Swanage all year, details of when the paddle steamer is sailing from the pier in the town harbour can be found on the events pages of the Swanage Railway's website. The cruises are operated by the owners of the paddle steamer and separate bookings and tickets are required for the train and the paddle steamer.

Tickets and details of sailings can be found on the paddle steamer's own website.

## Champagne Afternoon Tea

Why not treat yourself to a Champagne Afternoon Tea in the luxurious surroundings of the Devon Belle observation car? You will be greeted with a glass of champagne upon arrival, or a glass of orange juice if you prefer. A delicious afternoon tea will then be served at your seat on board the train as you travel along the railway. The menu for the afternoon tea is available on the event page on the railway's website and may vary. A vegan menu is available if you would prefer that option.

The large windows of the coach allow you an unapparelled view of the Purbeck scenery as well as the locomotive working right in front of the coach's large end windows on one leg of the return journey. The experience lasts for around one hour and involves a single return trip along the whole of the Swanage Railway.

Check the Swanage Railway website under the events pages for more details on dates the Afternoon Tea is served and costs. It is necessary to book the Champagne afternoon tea well in advance as it is quite popular.

A Prosecco version of this event is also available.

## Taster Driving Experience

Step aboard the footplate of a mighty steam locomotive as you take on the role of both driver and fireman of your own steam train on a complete round trip of the railway. Starting at Swanage, the expert friendly footplate crew will guide you through the intricacies of driving and firing a steam locomotive as you drive the train the five and half miles between Swanage and Norden and then fire the locomotive on the return trip, or fire the first leg and drive the second. There are ample opportunities for friends or family to take photographs with the steam locomotive at Swanage and Norden stations as a special keepsake of the day.

The experience lasts for approximately an hour on the footplate and is a special gift for a friend or relative. Actually why not just treat yourself? You know you deserve it.

The experience is available on certain days of the year, all of which are listed on the Taster Driver Experience page in the events listings on the Swanage Railway website. The driving experience begins at Swanage station, and it may be better on this occasion to park at the nearest long stay car park at Victoria Avenue (Post code BH19 1AP) which is a short ten minute or so walk from the railway station. There is no parking available at Swanage railway station.

Budding train drivers need to be able to climb unaided up and down from the steam engine cab and must be over the age of 18. You should also wear cotton clothes or overalls which you do not mind getting grubby for the experience. Long trousers and long sleeved tops and sturdy enclosed shoes are required. You will need to arrive at the booking office in Swanage station at least 30 minutes before the experience is due to begin for an introduction and safety briefing. The website page outlines all of the requirements for the experience, so check there for details and costs. Locomotives will be used from the railway's operating fleet and cannot be specified in advance.

It is well worth the effort though, operating a live, moving steam locomotive is an experience that will never be forgotten.

## Footplate Ride

Ever wondered what the footplate crew of a steam locomotive do and want to experience the sights, sounds and smells of a working steam engine? Then why not book a footplate ride on the railway?

The experience gives you the opportunity to travel in the cab of the steam locomotive on a service train on a complete round trip of the line from Swanage to Norden and return. The highly experienced engine crew will be happy to answer your questions and will point out interesting points along the journey. You will be able to see how the driver expertly controls the train and how the fireman keeps the boiler fed with coal and water as the locomotive works its way along the line. There is a lot involved in operating a steam engine, the driver needs to be planning ahead all the time and the fireman is not just throwing coal into the firebox. There is an art to both jobs, which you will see in action on your trip.

The experience lasts for around one hour but also includes all day travel on the Swanage Railway. Footplate trips are not available every day due to operational restrictions and other bookings, so it is necessary to book well in advance. The dates which the experience is available to book are advertised on the railway's website under the events and experiences tab.

## Class 33 Driving Experience

In 2024 the Swanage Railway began offering the opportunity of a driving experience on one of the heritage diesel electric locomotives based on the line. The Class 33s were built in the 1960s as part of British Railways' modernisation of traction across Britain. Mainly confined to the Southern Region of British Rail, the locomotives proved reliable, capable and popular with locomotive crews. The class was used on a wide variety of traffic, from freight to passenger trains, and were often found on the Swanage branch as well as the roadside line to Weymouth Docks.

The Class 33 driving experience is a fantastic opportunity to operate a modern diesel locomotive at work, under your own control. The experience allows you to drive your own train on a return trip between Swanage and Norden, and back. The friendly and experienced driver will show you how to drive the engine and will be happy to answer all your questions as you travel down the Swanage branch. The driving experience begins at Swanage station. It will be necessary to park in Swanage for this day out. The nearest long stay car park at Victoria Avenue

**Class 33** 'Crompton' D6515 (33012) *Lt Jenny Lewis RN* arriving at Corfe Castle with a service to Swanage on 22 September 2024. *Richard Marks*

(Post code BH19 1AP) is a short ten minute walk from the railway station. There is no parking available at Swanage railway station.

The driving experience lasts for approximately one hour. On the day you should arrive at least 30 minutes before your experience is due to start for a safety briefing and introduction. You should also wear overalls or clothes with long sleeves and trousers rather than shorts as well as sturdy enclosed shoes, which you don't mind getting grubby. Whilst the cab of a diesel locomotive is less dusty and oily than that on a steam locomotive, it is still a working railway engine. Anyone wishing to undertake the experience needs to be able to climb up and down from the cab unaided and be at least 18 years old.

There are plenty of opportunities to take photographs with the locomotive at Swanage and at Norden for family and friends of the 'driver'.

The experience is available on certain days, all of which are advertised on the Class 33 Driver Experience page under the Events and Experiences tab on the railway's website where you can also book your driving trip.

## Fish and Chip Specials

The railway runs Fish and Chip Specials on certain afternoons on steam hauled trains, although for operational reasons it is possible that the train may be diesel hauled on rare occasions. The trips begin at Norden, with fish and chips, a bottle of water and a baked sweet treat being served at the halfway point of the return journey at Swanage station. The trip lasts just over an hour and is a nice relaxed way to celebrate a birthday, other special event, or just to treat yourself to something a little extra. Tables are arranged in fours on heritage railway carriages, and so groups of two may be seated with another group of two at the same table.

Alternative meal options are available if you prefer not to have fish, and can be selected when booking tickets. Places can be limited and it is necessary to book in advance. The service is not operated by the Swanage Railway, bookings are taken and administered by a separate company. The booking button on the Swanage Railway's website for the Fish and Chip Specials will take you to the company's website who run the event where you can book.

## Children's Days

The railway often runs weekend events with a theme aimed at children. A fun filled day on the railway, with the opportunity to meet your favourite characters from children's television series is a joy. The days vary each year but are well advertised on the railway's website under the events and experiences tab. Keep an eye on the website, you may well find a perfect fun day out for all the family.

## Steam Galas

The railway frequently runs long weekend themed 'gala' events, usually operating between Friday and Sunday. The railway hosts visiting steam engines from other heritage railways and mainline steam operators over the weekend. The events see an intensive and varied train service, with many trains running each day. The opportunity to see giants of the steam age operating in tandem 'double-headed' on trains, or to see recreated freight trains or branch line trains from yesteryear is not to be missed.

Each year the railway runs a 'Winter Warm Up' gala in early January which is a great way to shift those post-Christmas winter blues. A smaller event than the summer and autumn steam galas, the event sees an intensive timetable with demonstration freight trains to see while you are waiting for your train makes this an enjoyable event.

The main big galas are usually run in the summer and autumn. These long weekends see the railway welcoming visiting locomotives and are themed to commemorate an anniversary, railway or industry related historical milestone. On occasion the theme is related to a large gathering of similar popular types of locomotives. In 2024 the railway hosted almost every surviving Southern Railway express passenger locomotive designed by Oliver Bullied. The Strictly Bulleid gala weekend saw an impressive eight of these mighty express passenger locomotives making for a spectacular weekend.

Other gala themes in the past have celebrated the Victorian period, the country branch line railways once so important to local communities, the 1940s, the 1960s and the old railway companies among many other interesting historical topics. Each year the gala weekend themes change as do the visitors that you can see working the trains during the event.

On some gala weekends the railway runs shuttle services past Norden along the branch to the boundary with Network Rail. There are no stations after Norden so it is not possible to alight from or join the train. The railway has no facility to run the locomotive round the train to the other end ready to return to Swanage. The trains are top and tail operated with an engine at each end.

The Summer Steam Gala usually runs in early June, whilst the Autumn Steam Gala is arranged during September or October. The dates, themes and visiting

**Class 33** 'Crompton', 33 111 is at the rear of a train heading to Norden where it will continue along the branch to the Swanage Railway's boundary with Network Rail. There is a steam locomotive on the front of the train. This 'top and tail' operation was due to there being no facility to run round at the boundary. The two red squares in the cab window indicate that this is the rear of the train, and are used by signallers as a safety check to ensure that the train is complete when it passes their signal box. *Mark Pollard*

engines are advertised in the railway's events pages on the website. Regular updates are posted on the railway's news pages on the website.

## Sunset Shuttle

During July and the first weekend of September, the railway runs an extended timetable in the evening between Swanage and Corfe Castle, calling at Harman's Cross on the journey. The train is a heritage diesel train, either a heritage DMU, or a rake of coaches hauled by one of the railway's resident heritage diesel locomotives. The evening Sunset Shuttle timetable begins at around 6:30pm on

Friday and Saturday evenings only. The shuttle additionally runs during the Purbeck Film Festival at the end of August, during the Swanage Folk Festival in early September and also in the evenings all week during the Swanage Regatta and Carnival week.

The trains start from Swanage, departing hourly until the last service at around 10:30pm. The first two trains from Swanage call at Norden, the remainder only call at Norden if requested via the train's guard. The return services leave Corfe Castle hourly between 7pm and 11pm (five minutes earlier from Norden when calling there).

The evening shuttle is covered by a special Sunset Shuttle ticket which allows unlimited travel on the shuttle after 6pm and the cessation of the day's normal timetable. It does not allow for travel on the trains during the day. The normal daytime return tickets and Freedom of the Line unlimited travel tickets do often allow for travel on the Sunset Shuttle, but check at the ticket office or online for details before travelling.

Note that the Purbeck Park Car Park closes in the late evening. The time the car park closes is clearly marked on the boards by the entrance.

The Swanage Railway Website details when the extended timetable is in operation and the fares to travel on it.

## Roads to Rail Steam Rally

The railways were not the only places that steam power was adopted for haulage of loads. The Roads to Rail Steam Rallies run during the middle of the summer celebrate that less glamourous but no less important locomotive, the traction engine. The event sees many beautifully restored privately owned traction engines, steam rollers, and showmen's engines gathered near Corfe Castle. Accompanied by miniature traction engines, the field is filled with the colourful sight of these heroes of the second industrial revolution which were as important to Britain's economy as their giant cousins on the railways. The rally also features fairground rides, all powered by steam showmen's engines, trade stalls, delicious food and excellent bars as well as live music.

The Swanage Railway runs an intensive train service over the weekend , including a special evening diesel service to get you back from Corfe Castle at the end of the day.

A family friendly day out not to be missed, the weekend is a chance to experience a part of life which is long gone.

## Beer Festival

The railway has run beer festivals, sometimes in conjunction with diesel gala weekends. Often held at Corfe Castle station in the old goods yard, the festival offers the chance to sample a huge variety of local ales and ciders as well as hot food. All of the beers and ciders are usually the product of smaller, local independent craft breweries and you might just find a new favourite. Just don't sample too many or you might not be able to tell them apart !

## Easter Egg Hunt

The railway has in the past run a special event over the Easter Weekend. Passengers joining the trains can collect an entry form at Norden, Corfe Castle and Swanage stations and colour in the Easter Egg whilst on the train. Once you have completed your work of art, hand it in to the Easter Egg Hunt stall on Norden or Swanage to claim a free prize.

## Victorian Weekend

To celebrate the pioneering era of railway building in Victorian times, the railway ran a Victorian weekend with two locomotives from the nineteenth century in steam and pulling trains. One, a South Eastern and Chatham Railway O1 Class freight locomotive of 1896 was a visitor from the Bluebell Railway in Sussex, the other was the resident L&SWR T3 Class express passenger locomotive of 1895 which returned to steam for the first time since 1948 in 2023. The two were accompanied by more modern engines in the form of mighty Bulleid designed West Country Class *Eddystone* and a mixed traffic go anywhere do anything locomotive, a U Class locomotive, both of which are resident on the line.

The Purbeck Mining Museum at Norden was also open and operating their narrow gauge line celebrating the Victorian narrow gauge railways that were so key to mining and industry during the nineteenth century.

## Diesel Gala

If steam is not really your thing, the Swanage Railway runs regular gala weekends using only diesel locomotives. The railway throbs with the power of diesel engines over the weekend with both resident locomotives and visitors from other heritage railways, and main line operators gracing the line for the weekend. Usually operating a three train service with up to nine locomotives in operation, depending upon availability, which swap over during the day and operate alone or in tandem with other locomotives, the weekend is a festival of modern traction and an opportunity to experience the spectacle of diesel engines. Many of these have long been withdrawn from the national railway and were a key part of the change from traditional steam traction to modern diesel and electric traction during the 1960s. Alongside these heritage diesel locomotives visitors from the train operators provide a glimpse of the power of the engines operating on Britain's railways in the twenty-first century, many being locomotives which can be uncommon in many parts of the country.

## The Polar Express Christmas Specials

Each year the railway runs a season of Polar Express Christmas trains in association with Polar Productions Ltd. The season runs between late November and Christmas Eve and must be booked in advance.

The trains depart from Swanage railway station and it is not possible to board the train at any other station. On this occasion it is best to park in Swanage; the nearest car park is in Victoria Road (Post Code BH19 1AP) which can be accessed from the A351. The car park is a ten minute walk from the railway station, there is no parking available at the railway station itself. The route is accessible but involves a short hill so visitors should leave extra time if you might need it.

The Polar Express Christmas Special consists of a return train ride on the Swanage Railway from Swanage station to the 'North Pole'. On board the train you can meet all your favourite characters from the movie and book, played by actors. There will be singing and dancing on the train in an interactive experience with the characters. Everyone will receive a cup of hot chocolate and a cookie on the train journey and a special present on the return journey from the 'North Pole'. The seats on the train are arranged in groups of four around a table, although a wheelchair accessible space is available on the train, details can be found on the event page on the railway's website. If you wish to share your trip with another family, it is advisable to make a single booking for everyone so you can sit together.

Visitors should arrive at Swanage station at least half an hour before the departure time of your booked train. Make sure to leave plenty of time for your journey to Swanage, as trains cannot be delayed for late arrivals.

The Polar Express is extremely popular and sells out quickly, although the railway does endeavour to add additional coaches to trains or even to run additional trains when they can, so if your preferred date is sold out do check back.

# WHY NOT STAY AWHILE? OTHER PLACES TO VISIT NEARBY

There are many more places to see and things to do while you are in Dorset so why not stay for longer for a weekend break, or perhaps even a week or two holiday in the Isle of Purbeck? Perhaps another day trip might be a pleasant escape, leaving the car at Norden and letting the train do the work.

There are many places to stay near the railway, and a little further afield. The county is well provided with affordable hotels and inns, as well as more luxurious and expensive hotels for that special weekend. There are many self-catering holiday cottages in some beautiful locations which can make a holiday a little different and memorable. The Visit Dorset website has many suggestions for places to stay, which are suitable for all budgets and tastes. The website can also help you find things to do and places to see.

## Bournemouth

Bournemouth is a little further away, but can be reached easily by road, rail and bus. The railway station, located on the edge of the town centre, is well served by regular trains to London, Reading, Birmingham, Southampton and the Midlands.

The town is the largest resort in Dorset, and boasts seven miles of unspoilt beaches, sandbanks, beautiful parks and gardens as well as a vibrant nightlife. There are plenty of places to eat and drink as well as to shop should you want to do so. The town boasts many of the well-known brands, but stepping into the Victorian arcades you find a mix of boutiques and independent shops.

The town has some fantastic entertainment venues. The Bournemouth International Centre hosts conferences and exhibitions as well as theatre and music whilst the Pavilion Theatre has a varied programme of shows all year round. The two venues present a wide selection of entertainment from children's shows and comedy to ballet and ice dancing. The town also has an ongoing series of events across the year.

There is a lot to do in Bournemouth. Find out more on the town's tourism website.

## Poole

Poole is a vibrant town with great restaurants and bars many of which are located on the waterfront. If shopping is your mission, then the town does not disappoint, with three inter-connected shopping areas with many of the high street brands located in the Dolphin Centre. The pedestrianised high street has an impressive array of independent shops which might just have that something different you are looking for.

The harbour, a working port, is the second largest natural harbour in the world after Sydney in Australia. You can often see a variety of ships in the harbour and it is possible to travel to Jersey and Guernsey in the Channel Islands as well as to France from Poole. Pleasure trips from the harbour provide a different view of the coast of Dorset and Poole Harbour. You could also catch a boat to the National Trust's Brownsea Island, home of the Scouting Movement and a variety of wildlife, including red squirrels.

Perhaps a day on the beach or exploring the area by bicycle might be what you are looking for. Poole is well situated to help you. Poole's three miles of award winning 'blue flag' Sandbanks beaches are amazing places to be at any time of year, whilst the 50 miles of cycle network centred on the town will suit the more adventurous.

Poole has a long time connection to the lifeboats which save lives around Britain's coast in all weathers every day. The Royal National Lifeboat Institution (RNLI), a charity which receives no government support, is headquartered in the town. A ninety minute tour will take you behind the scenes at the RNLI college where you can see how the volunteer lifeboat crews and lifeguards are trained. You can also stay in the RNLI hotel or enjoy a drink and something to eat in their bar and restaurant.

There are a variety of events in Poole throughout the year. Live music, arts festivals and open-air theatre are just some of what you could enjoy. The Tower

Park leisure complex contains a ten screen cinema, bowling alley and restaurants. Located out of town the park is well connected by bus, and also has a large free car park.

Poole is well connected by rail, services between Bournemouth and Weymouth calling regularly at the town centre station. Buses are also frequent and travel over a wide area.

There is so much more to do in Poole, find out more on Poole's official tourism website.

## Wareham

Wareham is a one of only a handful of Anglo-Saxon walled towns which remain in England. It is a pretty riverside town located where the rivers Piddle and Frome meet. With over 2,000 years of history to explore Wareham is worth a visit.

The town museum, located on the corner of North Street and East Street, is well worth a visit. It has displays explaining the geology and history of the town as well as an exhibition related to T.E. Lawrence (Lawrence of Arabia) who was stationed at Bovington Camp and lived nearby at his retreat, Clouds Hill. Why not also spend a little time walking the old Saxon town walls?

The walls, originally built to protect Wareham from Viking attack, now form the pleasant short walk around the town. Approximately a mile in length the walk takes around 45 minutes. There are slopes to get up onto the walls, but after that the walk is relatively level. A route leaflet about the walk can be downloaded from Dorset Council's website. Follow the links to 'Sport and Leisure' and then 'Walking'. The Wareham walk can be found under 'Walking in Purbeck.

The riverside quay at the bottom of the town has many events plus a weekly Saturday market where you can purchase local produce. It is the ideal place to have a picnic by the river, hire a boat, or just sit and watch the world go by for a while. Wareham has independent local retailers selling locally made products.

There are a wide choice of restaurants, pubs and cafes in the town, so you will be sure to find something tasty to eat. Wareham has you covered for everything from a simple sandwich to a romantic candlelit dinner.

Parking in Wareham is not plentiful, the main car park located in Howard's Lane (BH20 4NN) is very reasonably priced and whilst it is often quite busy a space can usually be found at most times of the day. Alternative parking is located across the road in Bonnets Lane East (BH20 4JN) on the odd occasion

**The view** from People's Viewpoint on the B3351 from Studland. Looking out across Studland and Godlingston Heath National Nature Reserve towards Brownsea Island with Poole in the distance behind it. *Richard Marks*

that Howard's Lane is full. The car parks will be very busy during the very popular Wareham Beer Festival in October.

The area south of Wareham is a large nature reserve, made of three separate reserves. Stoborough Heath, Arne Reedbeds and Hartland Moor. All are accessible by road from the A351 south of Wareham. The roads are narrow but have passing places. The reserves are great for walking and are peaceful places to enjoy nature and recharge. The Royal Society for the Protection of Birds has a visitor centre at Arne, which has a small entry charge, with a large car park and café. The RSPB offer a series of events and guided nature walks, you can even hire your own guide for a few hours (for parties of three or more people). Details can be found on the RSPB website from the 'Visit a reserve' drop down menu under the 'Days out' tab on the top of the home page.

**The coastal** path at Durlston Country Park and Nature Reserve. *Rosalind Marks*

The Hartland Moor heathland is owned by the National Trust and is well worth a visit for walking, although there is limited parking on the moors to help conserve the natural habitat. There is a lot to see though with many species of native British plants and wildlife being abundant. The moors have thriving populations of wild ponies, pigs and sheep which roam freely. The area's industrial history is not forgotten either. The remains of part of the route of the Middlebere Tramway which crossed the moors form a pleasant walk across the moors as far as Norden.

The area is well worth visiting whilst you are on the Isle of Purbeck.

## Wimborne Minster

Wimborne Minster is a picturesque and historic Dorset riverside town. The town dates back to before the Roman invasion. This rich history and its location on the banks of the rivers Stour and Allen makes Wimborne Minster a place well worth visiting. The town can be reached by bus or by car, but unfortunately not by rail. The town's railway station was closed in 1964.

Wimborne Minster church is the parish church for the area and has been an important part of the town for over 1300 years. The church is well worth a visit, the collection of quirky artefacts and the architecture of the building are a must see. The central tower and nave of the minster church were constructed during the Anglo-Saxon period, whilst the majority of the rest of the building is of Norman origin. Gothic architecture can be found around the church, added when the building was changed over time.

An interesting feature of the church is an astronomical clock which chimes every hour. Astronomical clocks contain special mechanisms and dials which display the relative positions of the sun, moon and zodiac constellations. The clock in the minster dates back to the fourteenth century. Although the current mechanism was put into the clock in 1792 and the case is Elizabethan, the dials and other parts of the clock are believed to be original. The clock operates an automaton

**Wimborne Minster.** *Mike Searle*

(known as a quarterjack) on the outside of the building which rings a bell with a hammer. Originally the figure of a monk, the quarterjack was replaced with the figure of a redcoat soldier during the Napoleonic Wars. The clock is recognised as being one of the most important examples of ancient working clocks in Europe.

The church is home to a chained library, one of only a handful which survive. Chained libraries were common from the Middle Ages until the eighteenth century. The books were chained to the shelves in their bookcases to prevent the books being stolen. The chains were long enough to allow the book to be taken to a nearby table to be read. Wimborne Minster's library, the second largest today, contains some especially rare books. A manuscript dated 1343, a book bound for Henry VIII and a pamphlet printed in 1495 are just a few of the highlights the library has to offer. The library is run by volunteers and is open to the public on weekdays, usually between 10.30 and 12.30 in the morning and 2.00 to 4.00 in the afternoon. As the library is run by volunteers it may not be open every day.

The town is well located for pleasant riverside walks, or as a base to explore the local countryside by bicycle. There are local nature reserves and dog-friendly walking routes for a relaxing hour or two away from the hustle and bustle of daily life.

Wimborne is a 'fairtrade' town and has local independent businesses selling a diverse range of products. Remember the days of the local record shop and the independent bookshop? You may well find them in Wimborne in the hidden courtyards and pedestrianised parts of the town centre. Ideal for finding something special or maybe even that album you've been looking for. You never know!

The town has many restaurants and pubs offering everything from a delicious full English breakfast to a romantic meal in a fine dining restaurant. Some of the eateries offer take out options that you can enjoy on your day out. Regular food festivals and farmers markets are a part of the town's events calendar all of which provide a chance to sample local produce.

Wimborne model town presents a 1:10 scale model of the town as it was in the 1950s set in delightful gardens. The model town contains some amazing buildings including a working model of the minster's quarterjack, a telephone box with a ringing phone, and much more. The model town has a model of the model in 1:100 scale and a model of the model of the model in an even smaller scale. Why not ask to see this fine example of the model makers art? There is also an opportunity to become a train driver on the model town's model railway, or to play a game of crazy golf while you are there. The café serves a selection of hot and cold drinks, homemade cakes, and lunches. The model town is open on most days of the year.

The Museum of East Dorset is located in a Grade II* listed historic town house in the heart of Wimborne. The museum tells the story of the people who lived in and around Wimborne. With a selection of galleries recreating rooms from a seventeenth century hall to a Victorian kitchen the museum provides a fascinating glimpse into the way we used to live.

## Kingston Lacey

Located just three miles from Wimborne Minster, the country house at Kingston Lacy (BH21 4EA), in the care of the National Trust, is a must see part of a trip to the area. The house was built in the seventeenth century in the style of an Italian palace by the Bankes family who owned huge swathes of Dorset for over 400 years.

The collections that can be seen in the house include an impressive collection of paintings by Rubens, Van Dyke, Titian and Breughel. The collection of ancient

**Kingston Lacy** House. *Richard Marks*

Egyptian artefacts is one of the largest private collections in Britain, all of which were collected by William John Bankes during his travels across Egypt in 1818. The Spanish Room is not to be missed. The gilded leather and ceiling were brought to Kingston Lacy from the Contarini Palace in Venice and are breath taking.

The house is set in 8,500 acres of parkland with more formal gardens located in the grounds of the house including a Japanese Garden complete with Japanese tea-house. The cherry blossom can be impressive during the spring and whilst only fleeting is well worth a visit to see.

The gardens and park are open between 9.30am and 5.00pm on most days of the year as is the Stable Café serving a selection of hot and cold drinks, home-made cakes and lunches. The house is usually open for a shorter period of time each day, usually between 10.30am and 4.00pm, although last entry is at 3.00pm. On occasion the house may be closed although the grounds are still open except on Christmas Day when all but the Badbury Rings Car Park is closed to visitors. Entry to the house is limited and visitors should ask for a timed ticket upon arrival. At the time of writing it does not appear to be possible to book visits to the house in advance. More information about the house and grounds as well as entry prices and opening times can be found on the National Trust's website.

## Studland Bay

Studland is located at the end of the road from Corfe Castle. The B3351 road from Corfe Castle leaves the A351 just opposite the castle before you reach the village, passing under the railway bridge carrying the Swanage Railway. There are also roads from Studland to Swanage if you are travelling from there.

The pretty village of Studland is located on a peninsula which projects into Poole Harbour. There are places to eat and drink in the village serving a variety of food. The Studland to Poole ferry leaves from just outside the village.

Studland is famous for its long stretches of sandy beaches in the bay, and can be very busy in the summer. There are four beaches, Shell Bay, Knoll Beach, Middle Beach and South Beach. The beaches are owned by the National Trust who have provided a large car park at each, which are free for National Trust members. Adjacent to the car park at Knoll Beach is a visitor centre, shop and well-appointed café, all operated by the National Trust. There are no lifeguards at the beaches.

**The beaches** at Studland Bay. *Rosalind Marks*

One of the beaches has been designated a nudist beach, so is worth bearing in mind if you decide to walk the beach in the Poole direction.

Visible to the right as you walk onto Knoll Beach is a long headland at the end of which are two separated large rock stacks, which are known as Old Harry Rocks.

Studland Bay is an excellent place to begin a coastal walk. For the more adventurous, Knoll Beach at Studland is the beginning of the 630 mile South West Coath Path which ends at Minehead on the north coast of Somerset, having passed around the entire coast of Cornwall. For those with less demanding walking ambitions, Studland has pleasant short and medium length walks. An easy one mile walk from Studland will take you up the coast to Old Harry Rocks and is worth doing, just to enjoy the natural environment through which the walk passes.

As with the rest of the Isle of Purbeck, the area around Studland has a lot of history to enjoy. The bay, which can be glimpsed on a walk along the beaches has a connection with D-Day. During the Second World War, the area was viewed as being a potential site for an invasion from Europe. The beaches were closed and fortified to prevent such unwelcome visitors, a far cry from today when everyone is welcome.

In 1942 the nearby village of Goathorn was evacuated as the area was to be used by the army for training and like its neighbour at Tyneham the villagers never returned. The village is now long lost to nature and little remains other than the pier which used to serve one of the many clay tramways which crossed the heath. Later the area was used for the preparations for the Operation Overlord invasion of Normandy, better known as D-Day. The beaches and local villages were used as a training area for troops before the landings. At Knoll Beach you can still visit one of the remnants of the preparations, Fort Henry.

**Studland Bay,** looking towards Old Harry Rocks. *Richard Marks*

**Plaque on** Swanage railway station commemorating the American soldiers billeted in the town during the training for the D-Day landings undertaken locally. Many of the soldiers who left Swanage bound for the invasion never went home, and their sacrifice for freedom should never be forgotten. *Richard Marks*

Fort Henry is a Grade II listed observation bunker built in 1943 which overlooks Studland Bay. The bunker was visited on 18 April 1944 by Winston Churchill; King George VI; General Dwight D. Eisenhower; Field Marshal Bernard Montgomery and Admiral Louis Mountbatten. The men were there to observe Exercise Smash, the largest live firing exercise of the entire war. The bunker is now owned by the National Trust and is part of a very interesting Studland Beach Second World War Walk. The walk starts at the Middle Beach car park.

The heathland behind the beach is, like most of the Isle of Purbeck, a haven for native wildlife, including all six British reptiles. There are designated trails through the dunes and woodlands, where you might see local deer, many species of birds and insects, as well as an abundance of wild flowers.

More information about the beaches, things to do, and the history of the area can be found on the National Trust's website.

## Lulworth Cove and Durdle Door

Lulworth Cove (BH20 5RQ) and the nearby coast are part of the Jurassic Coast UNESCO World Heritage site. The sheltered bay and pebble beach provide a great place to stop for a while and enjoy the seaside. The sedimentary rock laid down over 150 million years ago contains a wealth of fossils giving palaeontologists and visitors a glimpse of the prehistoric past. The rock has been folded in places, and the sedimentary layers no longer lie neatly on top of one another. The formations visible on the cliffs show the layers of rock, now vertical, providing the visitor with a stunning appreciation of the turbulent geological past of the planet although the tourist websites and leaflets advise visitors not to climb or sit under the cliffs. There was a major landslip early in 2024 which blocked the beach about half way round. The Cove remained open, but the website advised caution around the base of the cliffs. The rock formations can be seen from the other side of the cove, however. Check the website for updates before visiting or ask in the visitor's centre before heading down to the Cove.

**Lulworth Cove.** *Rosalind Marks*

**Durdle Door,** seen from the Jurassic Coast path over the cliffs from Lulworth Cove. The arch is a natural formation caused by sea erosion of the natural limestone. *Saffron Blaze*

The Cove is provided with a large car park which is open 24 hours. Adjacent to the car park there is a well-appointed visitor centre, usually open between 10.00am and 5.00pm (4.00pm in winter). It is closed on Christmas Day. The interesting displays and animations in the visitor centre clearly explain the geology of the area and there is also a helpdesk which will assist you with anything from geological maps to the time of the tides.

Lulworth Cove has several places to eat and access to the beach can be found via a gentle wide path and slipway. For the more adventurous the coastal path leaves the car park and heads to the top of the cliffs, where you can walk to famous landmarks at Durdle Door and Stair Hole. The path is quite steep and you should bring sturdy footwear if you are intending to walk the coast path. The cliffs can be crumbling in places due to the effects of coastal erosion, so care is needed. An all-terrain Tramper Mobility Scooter is available to hire but needs to be booked in advance.

Lulworth Cove is extremely popular and during the summer months can be very busy. More details about Lulworth Cove and how to book the mobility scooter can be found on the Visit Dorset website. More details about the Lulworth Estate, of which the Cove is part, can be found on their website.

## Tyneham Village

The village where time stopped, Tyneham (BH20 5QF) is the ghostly village where only memories of the people who once lived there remain. Once a vibrant local community, the village, like that at Goathorn, was evacuated in 1943 as the area was needed for military training. When the war ended in 1945, the villagers were not allowed to return and Tyneham has remained deserted ever since. On days when the village is open to visitors there is car parking (paid for by a suggested donation advertised on the notice boards) and toilet facilities.

The village is part of the British Army training establishment and Armoured Fighting Vehicle Gunnery School based at the nearby Bovington Camp.

**Tyneham Village.** Some of the buildings have begun to become overgrown. Where once there were gardens, now there are trees and ferns. *Richard Marks*

**Post Office** Row in the abandoned Tyneham Village. *Richard Marks*

Bovington is home to the Royal Armoured Corps and also to the Tank Museum. Access to Tyneham is limited on days when the army is training. The local roads to the area are closed for operational and safety reasons as the area is used for training armoured fighting vehicle crews, with tanks often undertaking live firing gunnery exercises on Lulworth Ranges to hone the skills of the crews.

A visit to the village can be thought provoking. Many of the original buildings still stand, but are derelict. The Row, a row of four terraced houses and Tyneham Farm which has now been partly restored give a sense of what life might have been like for the people who lived in the villages. The church and the old school buildings are still intact, both now contain exhibitions about the village and its people. A visit it most highly recommended.

The main road is quite narrow, and whilst perfectly fine for a car, coaches, larger minibuses and camper vans are not permitted. More details can be found on the Visit Dorset website.

**Ruined cottages** at Tyneham Village. *Richard Marks*

The village is generally open on weekends and bank holidays, but it is advisable to check before travelling to avoid disappointment. The dates when the village can be visited can be found on the UK Government website.

## The Tank Museum

Home to what is probably one of the world's best collections of armoured vehicles, The Tank Museum (BH20 6JG) is a great place to spend a day. The museum is not just for tank fans and military historians. It brings the story of the tank and those that served in them vividly to life through a series of interpretative displays. The tank was a British invention and the museum has not only the first tank to see service in the British army, the First World War Mark I Heavy Tank of 1916, but also the prototype British tank that started it all. A prototype of the first tank with a turret, the French FT17, is also on display in the museum. Located within Bovington Camp, which alongside Lulworth Camp form Bovington Garrison,

**Inside the** Tank Museum with a Centurion tank nearest the camera, with a Second World War Churchill tank behind. Lurking in the distance is one of the few surviving German Panther tanks. *Richard Marks*

the museum is appropriately situated alongside the British army's working tank arm, the Royal Armoured Corps. During the week it is highly likely that you will be able to see modern tanks working around the base. The roads around the camp and museum have viewing points where visitors can park and watch the impressive modern tanks being put through their paces.

The displays of over 300 impressive military vehicles, which includes some strange prototypes, represents the battles of every conflict since the First World War. From the mud of Flanders in 1916 to the Normandy Beaches and the deserts of Iraq, the story of the tank and the brave men and women who served, and still serve in them, is brought to life. The museum features interactive displays suitable for everyone. A fascinating display covers the history of the tank in movies, from the very earliest times to recent blockbusters such as *Kelly's Heroes* and *Fury*.

**British FV432** Armoured Personnel Carrier demonstrating in the Tank Museum's arena. *Richard Marks*

T.E. Lawrence, wishing to avoid recognition, served in the Royal Tank Corps between 1923 and 1925 as T.E. Shaw before rejoining the Royal Air Force which he had left in 1923 after his true identity was exposed, Lawrence having enlisted as J.H Ross in 1922. Lawrence was killed in a motorcycle accident in 1935 near his retreat Clouds Hill, on one of the approach roads to Bovington Camp. The tank museum has a fascinating display related to Lawrence, which includes one of his Brough Superior motorcycles. There is also an interesting display related to the use of horses in war, the predecessors to the armoured cars which followed. There is an opportunity to go inside some of the vehicles in the museum, and on occasion the museum offers tank rides in the display arena.

There is a café in the museum's Tamiya Hall at the rear of the museum next to the soft play area, where you can get refreshment surrounded by some modern tanks. The restaurant is on the mezzanine level near the entrance. It can be accessed via steps at the entrance, which also has a lift, or by a ramp which can be reached by entering the museum and following the wall round to the left. It is open from 10.00am until 5.00pm and offers hot and cold drinks and a range of light snacks, pasties and sandwiches and salads. There is also a delicious range of reasonably priced hot meals and homemade cakes. There are also indoor and outdoor picnic areas if you prefer.

The museum runs special events, during which it can become quite busy. The Christmas fair is particularly popular as is the annual model show. Each year the museum runs events at which you can see tanks and armoured vehicles demonstrating in the tank museum's arena. The two events are very popular and require a separate ticket from the usual museum entry.

Before you leave the museum be sure to visit the well-stocked shop which has a variety of gifts and souvenirs and a wide range of clothing, books, toys and models suitable for all budgets.

More information about opening times, entrance prices and the special events can be found on the museum's website.

## Clouds Hill

Clouds Hill (BH20 7NQ) was the retreat belonging to T.E. Lawrence. The property is now in the care of the National Trust and is as Lawrence left it. The light levels inside are quite low to protect the decoration and furniture from the effects of sunlight so you might wish to arrange a visit during the summer months. The shed where Lawrence kept his much loved motorcycles, one of

**Clouds Hill,** *Carol Walker*

which is now on display in the Tank Museum, now contains an interesting display about his life. The Tank Museum is located only a short distance away from Clouds Hill and it is more than possible to combine visits to both on the same day.

It is necessary to book in advance as the property is quite small. Bookings are timed. There is an introductory tour presented by one of the National Trust's knowledgeable volunteers every 30 minutes which you might want to join. As always entry is free for National Trust members. Opening times vary during the year, and on some dates the property is closed to visitors. Check opening times, prices and book a visit on the property's page on the National Trust website.

## Monkey World

Monkey World (BH20 6HH) ape sanctuary is located very close to the tank museum. The sanctuary was first set up by Jim Cronin in 1987 to provide a safe home for abused Spanish beach chimpanzees and was operated by Jim and his wife Dr Alison Cronin, who continues to run the sanctuary today.

The park today works with foreign governments to stop the illegal trade in apes and monkeys smuggled out of Africa and Asia. It also aims to provide a safe home for apes and monkeys who have been smuggled. Monkey World hosts the biggest community of Chimpanzees outside of Africa, which are formed into four social groups. The park is also home to three groups of Orangutans, both Bornean and Sumatran which are now endangered in the wild due to loss of habitat.

With communities of five species of gibbons and fourteen species of monkey, the park provides an opportunity to visit some of our closest genetic relatives, and to appreciate them. Many of the residents of the park are real characters who you may have seen on the television series *Monkey Life* which is in its fifteenth series in 2024.

Why not support the valuable work of the Ape Rescue Centre by paying them a visit? It is a day out you won't forget. Monkey World is open every day apart from Christmas Day between 10.00am and 5.00pm. There is an entrance fee for the park, which varies by the number in your party. The park also offers a discounted rate for booking made online. To find out more about the park, the work of the rescue centre and entry prices go to the Monkey World website.

## Purbeck Film Festival

The festival started in 1996 with special screenings of movies at the Mowlem cinema in Swanage and the Rex cinema in Wareham to celebrate a century of cinema. Supported by the British Film Institute the festival has gone from strength to strength. In 1997 the Purbeck Film Festival received a grant from the National Lottery which allowed it to not only screen twenty-one films but to buy the Rex Cinema. The Rex is a valuable example of the cinemas that were once common across Britain but which have been replaced by the large out of town multiplexes we are so familiar with today. A visit to the Rex is not only a great way to enjoy a movie but also a heritage experience in its own right.

The festival, now an independent charity, offers support to local communities across Purbeck, allowing films to be accessible to everyone. The festival puts on affordable outdoor summer screenings at Corfe Castle, in the castle itself, Durlston Country Park and other venues. The screenings at Corfe Castle are a great way to take in a movie in a unique environment with the nearby heritage railway providing a great way to get to the village.

**The Rex** Cinema in Wareham, 11 June 2012. *Mike Finn*

The festival runs the Purbeck Shorts competition, giving new film makers a platform on which to showcase their talent. Providing an open and inclusive environment which attracts film makers from all over the world, culminating in a screening at the Mowlem cinema in Swanage during the final weekend of the Purbeck Film Festival. There is also an Autumn Film Festival in the last two weeks of October, showcasing all that is great about movies on the big screen.

More details about the festival can be found on the Purbeck Film Festival Website

## Visit Dorset

The county has a lot to offer the visitor, more than can be presented in a book of this size. The Visit Dorset website is an excellent way to plan a visit to all of the interesting places the county has to offer. Start your trip by spending some time at https://www.visit-dorset.com/ you never know what you might find.

Enjoy exploring Dorset and the Swanage Railway.

# SOURCES AND FURTHER READING

The following, alongside site visits, were used in the research for this book.


Jackson, B.L. *Castleman's Corkscrew including The Railways of Bournemouth and Associated Lines: Volume One: The Nineteenth Century* (Oakwood Press, 2007).

Jackson, B.L. *Castleman's Corkscrew including The Railways of Bournemouth and Associated Lines: Volume Two: The Twentieth Century and Beyond* (Oakwood Press, 2007).

Jackson, B.L., *Swanage: 125 Years of Railways* (Oakwood Press, 2010).

Legg, Chris, *Fayle's Tramways: Clay Mining in Purbeck* (Twelveheads Press, 2016).

Nock, O.S., *The London and South Western Railway* (Ian Allen, 1966).

St. John Thomas, David, *A Regional History of the Railways of Great Britain. Volume 1: The West Country* (David and Charles, 1981).

Stanier, Peter, *Discover Dorset: The Industrial Past* (Dovecote Press, 1998).

Thomas, Jo, *Discover Dorset: Stone Quarrying* (Dovecote Press, 1998).

Williams, R.A., *The London and South Western Railway. Volume 1: The Formative Years* (David and Charles, 1968).

Williams, R.A., *The London and South Western Railway. Volume 2: Growth and Consolidation* (David and Charles, 1973).


Various files from the National Archives were examined including papers from AN177, BT285, MT6, and MT124.

# INDEX